HELLO, WELCOME TO M
HOPEFULLY, YOUR

Tracey x

To you, the parent/carer that didn't ask for this life and is going to give it everything you have.
To the parent/carer who thinks they can't do this but trust me, you can.
To the parent/carer who thinks they are alone, you aren't, I can assure you.

To my husband and kids... this is my escape away from you so don't bug me, thanks.

Contents

Introduction

INTRODUCTION

I complain a lot, like **a lot**. Although I complain a lot I am a strong believer that if you have a complaint, don't just put it out there without a solution. No solution means your complaint was completely useless. So, this book is the point of no return for me. I am done complaining, banging my drum, hoping that someone will step in and make a book just like this for those early days and instead decided, frig it. I'll do it.

I will pre-warn you now that my grammar is horrendous at times, my words can be colourful and that I am in deed a mackem/northerner. This means along the way I will probably have to give you some sort of dictionary of my slang as to be honest, it is pretty awful... but hey ho! Let's crack on!

This book is a mixture of my story, informative bits and bobs and of course... extracts from my daughter, Delilah. My hope for the book is to help you, the reader, feel more empowered to start sooner than later looking for support within the SEND world and to get a head start. I also want you to know, you're not alone.

Welcome to the wonderfully special club, that no one asks to be in.

Chapter **1**

HEY THERE, DELILAH

From birth to what the actual f**k?

It had been two years of trying. Two whole years of pregnancy tests, negatives and worry. What if it is just not supposed to be? What if we were just destined to have two. I was grateful for two, but we were a blended family and I so desperately wanted Dan to feel what I had felt twice before. That feeling of hope and joy. The smell of a new born baby, the hugs and overwhelming love that comes with them.

And then, it finally happened. We got that positive test. Then followed the usual drs appointment to confirm the pregnancy, just to then be given the devastating news that it just wasn't supposed to be. What had been there before was now gone, and I gave in. We had given in. We were very early pregnant as far as I can gather, there was no big announcements, just me and dan ecstatically happy then all of a sudden, low and hurt. We stuck together, kept our heads down and decided what would be would be. No more trying, no more exhausting conversations, just him and I... against the world.

Just as we gave in, just as we started to start living again, there she appeared. Like a little shock out of nowhere, she was there. From day one, she was trouble.

I was six weeks pregnant when I started to bleed. I was scared and nervous but had to be check over. That little dot was there but no heartbeat. Please not again. We were told not to worry, that this is common, to come back in two weeks. Two bloody weeks, can you imagine? Two whole weeks of not knowing whether or not everything was going to be ok. We walked on egg shells, Dan was so protective of me and kept a very close eye on me, even sneezing was something he considered to be highly dangerous.

The two weeks had passed, and there she was, our little fighter. A strong heartbeat, little movements and all was well, we thought.

■■

Oh wait, maybe I should rewind a bit...

This was not my first pregnancy, I have two older children. I have a girl, who at the time of writing this, is sixteen and making her way to college in just two months! Scary stuff! And then there is our boy, the middle child, the little lost boy who is dominated by girls and he is thirteen.

I don't mention the names of my older children, or divulge

too much information because they are of course teenagers. Being a teenager in this day and age is tough so please don't think when reading my book that they have been lost, abandoned or locked in a cupboard under the stairs, because trust me they aren't. Mainly because we don't have a cupboard under the stairs and because quite frankly they are quieter apart than they are together.

■■

I was sixteen, yep, you read that right, when I gave birth to my first child, my daughter. She was born in November 2004 and I turned 17 in the December. I grew up quick, from giving birth one year, moving out the following and then we got married the year following that. It wasn't a fairytale, it wasn't all wonderful and 'meant to be'. It felt like it was expected of me, I had got pregnant to my 'high school sweetheart'. We had been together for near enough the whole entire time I was at secondary school so it was normal natural progression to move out together and get married. Our marriage lasted in reality, about three weeks. We were young, we grew up and grew apart. On paper, our marriage lasted a lot longer, getting divorced is quite a process!

So, back to the story. This was my first pregnancy, everything went well throughout labour and birth. I have nothing really to report except giving birth to, what was at the time, a little tiny baby of 6lb 14ozs. She was perfection, I learnt fast how to be a 'mam' and to grow up, stand on my own two feet and how to be strong in whatever life throws at you.

Following on from the break down of my marriage, I moved on. It's a longer story I can make very, very short in one sentence. Everyone has one of those moments when you look back and think "what the fuck was I thinking then?"... well that, that was my second 'serious'... if you can call it that... relationship. But, it did give me my son. My weird and wonderful son, who I also had no issues with, except his delivery was SO quick. Like I went into labour at 12am and he was here by 8am the next morning, kinda quick. He was a huge 9lb and 1oz... I don't know where the big baby come from because at the time I was barely a size 8 (not so much now, boo hoo) so there was definitely no way of hiding a pregnancy!

So that is that, that is my history of births and messy situations. I had two children. I knew my stuff, I knew what to expect and wasn't at all afraid of welcoming another little bundle into our home. I was soo excited! This was it, our family would be complete.

■■

Throughout my pregnancy I had a very strong feeling of something not being 'right'. It is definitely a feeling that can't be explained well enough to give you a complete understanding but I knew that there was trouble, something wasn't right and I was desperate for someone to confirm it.

Bless Dan though, he was soo cautious as he had never done this before. Every time I felt a little 'off' he would head home to look after me, run me to hospital and care for me so I didn't feel alone. We also decided to hire a Fetal Doppler in order to hear her heartbeat every now and again. I do not advise this, at all. At times it caused more worry than good because at times we couldn't find her, we weren't trained and didn't know what we were doing. More hassle than good.

We had two 3D scans also, partially because I was too damn excited to have the option this pregnancy and partially down to the concerns I had. They were amazing! We found out at 16 weeks that our baby was a girl. We had listed lots of names for both sexes but knowing what sex she was didn't make it any easier to choose.

Out of the blue one day Dan said, "What about Delilah?"

Hmmmm what about Delilah? Honestly, didn't not like it, just didn't love it. I couldn't get my head around calling my bump Delilah, and neither could anyone I told. Then one day a friend explained how our local football club, SAFC, had a mascot called Delilah. Dan was an avid fan at the time and it all made sense to me that this is where he had gotten her name from... yet he still denies this to this day.

Named picked, and loving the song any way I played 'hey there, Delilah' every time I felt I needed rest or if I was feeling a little worried about her. This became our song, our little moments together. The calm before all of the storm that was heading our way.

Throughout my whole 41 weeks of pregnancy I visited the pre natal day clinic a good handful of times. I spoke to my midwife often and felt I always needed extra support. I'd have moments where I would spot, bleed or feel a reduction in her movements. I would have days of cramps and aches and pains, I was sure my body was trying to tell me something. Someone, somewhere was trying to give me the heads up.

Motherly instinct was in full mode, but only I could hear it, feel it and couldn't do anything about it.

"She is fine" they would say, "her movements aren't considered worrying" they'd say, "she's a good size too, a nice juicy size baby" they meant she was huge. They were just too polite to say it, and because of her size they had given me two sweeps in the hopes of inducing my labour naturally. They didn't know Delilah though, was she heck moving for anyone!

The day finally came, I went into labour on the 15TH March 2012. I was in labour a full 24hrs with what seemed like zero issues, or anything to be overly concerned about. Granted, she didn't cry like other babies, was quite blue for 24hrs and had to have her airways cleared which had meant dad couldn't cut the cord but otherwise she seemed wonderful. She was amazing and all ours. All 9lb and 3ozs of baby... they didn't lie when they said she would be juicy! Our family was complete. Me, him and three, what more could I ask for?

■■

Delilah was born with a striking birth mark on her face, as you can see in the picture. It is a very obvious one that needed to be checked while we were in hospital.

"I knew it!" I thought to myself, I knew there was something.

"She's fine mr and mrs huggins, no cancer detected, it is definitely a birth mark and not a mole and that mark there? Yea that, that is a third nipple. Also, her skin is very dry, this is because your baby was in there a little longer, so she was 'overcooked' if you like. Once you start bathing her, apply some baby oil afterwards and it will clear up in no time! You are free to get sorted and head home"

Wow, if only they knew.

Let's fast forward a bit, because quite frankly up until this point it was your average new born story. Shortly after giving birth we went to our local church and booked Delilahs Christening and our wedding for the following year. Delilahs Christening was booked for that October and our wedding the following June. Life was great really, normal actually...

We didn't sleep great. She ate, I cried, she pooped, I cleaned it up and that was our days. We would play Ed Sheeran 'drunk' on repeat on the day's she wouldn't nap, this would soothe her off and dad too. I can remember the first night we had her home and she slept all the way through the night, both me and Dan had jumped up the following morning to check she was breathing. Babies don't sleep this well on their first night home!

All the while her skin was getting no better. Delilah was very dry, I would bathe her, apply cream and within an hour she would be dry again. It felt like we were chasing our tail but we never gave in, we just kept trying.

Then, it was as if time had stopped still. Delilah had started to smile, started to waffle and coo... but that was it. As a mam of two other children, I knew where she should have been with her development.

And I know, before anyone says it 'you should never compare kids' but come on, who can say they've NEVER compared children, compared themselves or had a situation where they have really second guessed something. If you say you haven't, I don't believe you.

My niece had been born exactly 11 days before Delilah, there was no way I was going to be able to go through those early years without comparing the children because I am human. We all are.
Now though, I was at a point of predicament, one I had never expected to be in and one I certainly wasn't prepared for. Do I go to have Delilah checked over OR am I being an over-reactor?

██

So here I am, just me and D sat in a drs waiting room awaiting to be seen. Nothing out of the usual, I wasn't concerned or stressed, I just thought we will be in and out and I will be back for school run.

And that is exactly what happened. We spoke about her not showing any signs of attempting to sit up, the fact that she cried a lot when it was warm and that there was no signs of her skin getting any better. The Dr had said on the fact of how dry she was, she would pop her name on the waiting list for dermatology in order to have her skin checked over and I was simply told the good old line of...

'All kids are different, they all develop differently, I am sure she is fine'.

And off we went, it was Thursday 2ND August.

On the morning of Saturday the 4TH August we were hand delivered a letter from our local hospital paediatrician asking us to contact him first thing Monday morning to discuss Delilahs MRI that was booked for Tuesday morning.

Erm, what the f**k?

Hang on a minute? Did I blink and miss something?

The Dr didn't tell me she was referring Delilah? She didn't tell me she was concerned... she... she... had been calm... she said everything will be fine... she lied. We were guttered.

The day I had awaited for during my pregnancy, the one I was oh so sure was over, that I had just been nervous... had just hit me like a tonne of bricks.

I should have known. How did I not know?

I told you
she was a
'juicy' baby,
look at

The birth
mark that seemed to
be our only concern at birth.

Hello,

I'm hoping that by this point in the book you have already found something that may resonate with you. As much as these pages are my story, I feel they are important for me, to show you, that I was once exactly where you the new parent carer is right now.

Spoiler — it is less doom and gloom further on!

Tracey

x

Dear Parents Of Children with additional Needs,

This is my open letter to you, a parent that has been through 9 years of this world.

You are still just mam and dad. You just become a different type...

I am here to tell you lot's of things but firstly I want to say you will one day be ok. If you are not ok right now - that is ok. Do not let anyone tell you otherwise. You have just went through an experience that only a few go through. Learning their child has additional needs, a certain syndrome, condition, life long illness or like us, no diagnosis at all. This experience will 100% change you, your family, your love life, your friendships and your view of the world.

As it stands right now, things are shit. You will no doubt feel lost, confused, guilt and even grief. Grief is something that happens and you won't even see it coming. Grief hits you in the face, heart and head at great speed. You will grieve for the child you envisioned on that day when you saw that test say 'pregnant'. In that moment you may have saw yourself out with the kids, running to the park, pulling them down from the stairs and chasing them round the house like me shouting at them. But that didn't come and maybe that child won't. This is completely normal feelings to have.

Things will not get easier, they will get tougher but trust me when I say you will adapt. You will grow into a person you never even knew existed. That strong person inside you that can make quick decisions, negotiate appointments and learn what certain medical terminology will step forward, into the light and claim their moment. Because we all have them you know, that person in us and they WILL show up I promise you. It may not be today, tomorrow or three years from now but they will appear. It took me 7 years and 8 months to realise I was here all along.

At times you will forget yourself, take beauty in the small things - the collateral beauty if you like, and embrace and celebrate those little things as if all your Christmas's have come at once. These are the moment's that no one else gets to have. These are the moments that make this world, beautiful, wonderful and overwhelming. The fine line between too much crazy and too much love.

So here is my advice to you, take the small things and hold on to them, tightly. Pick your battles, you can't win them all in one day, NO ONE can. Find your own path, not everyones navigates the same way through this world. Times will be overwhelming, take a moment and let them be. Cry when you need to cry. You will get called superhuman on numerous occasions, this is a compliment - don't scowl at people. You will get asked "how do you do it all?" Don't harm these people - they are being polite and are well meaning. Laugh as much as you can. Laugh when you can, have fun when you can and take the help offered for you to do this.

Do all of the above.... And you probably won't be as you used to be... but you will be OK.

From me to you, welcome to the wonderfully special club, that no one asks to be in...

Tracey x

Chapter 2

OK, BUT WHAT NEXT?

Well, that escalated quickly...

So, here we were. Tuesday August 7th, 2012. Delilah was 144 days old and we were sat on a ward in the hospital awaiting for Delilah to be sedated in order to have her very first MRI.

We were terrified. We had gone from happy in our new baby bubble, as a family of five, to being sat in a hospital room completely unaware of what the fuck was going on.

Delilah had projectile vomited the pre medication up all over herself and Dan... It was ok the nurses had said, as she had swallowed enough to take affect. Delilah dosed off to sleep without a care in the world, her little sleepy body was popped into the ward pram and we went down for her MRI.

After removing our jewellery etc we were allowed to go in with her, we stood back and watched as they made her comfortable in this huge machine in a large empty room. We were ushered behind the protective glass into a smaller room covered in screens and warned what we were about to hear would be loud and scary BUT Delilah wouldn't feel or hear a thing.

We just stood there. Shell shocked.

It was probably only a few minutes long but it felt as if it had been forever... just watching our tiny little baby, in this huge polo shaped machine, completely unaware that anything was even happening.

Once over, we packed up her toys and headed off home.

"You should hear from the doctor within a week for your results!"

■■

Almost two weeks had passed and we had heard nothing. I was stressed, Dan was stressed and there was a constant uneasy feeling. Everyone, and I mean everyone had stated "she will be fine" or "it will be nothing!"

And quite often I got told "every kid develops differently you know!", as if I didn't know, or hadn't heard that before!

So here I am, two weeks after what seemed to be the worst day of my life and I was late. My period hadn't arrived and I was scared. I love my kids, all three of them but I sure as hell didn't want another added to the mix!

So, I headed off to the doctors. I wasn't pregnant, PHEW! But there had to be something else, there had to be a reason I was so late.

Casually the doctor had turned to me and simply asked "any reason you maybe stressed, Mrs Huggins?"

Wow, I bet she wish she hadn't asked! I rambled for about ten minutes about the weeks previous, the concerns I had and the fact that no-one had contacted us yet to put us out of our misery.

"Oh! Yes, that probably will be it!" She said so bluntly.

"But, I can check to see if the results are in if you like? After all she is your child and you are her next of kin"

I was so elated to have someone listen to me, and to give me the results that I had never second guessed what they may actually say.

■■

The room was almost silent. The only sound was that of the doctors heavy typing on those big old keyboards they all seem to have.

I patiently waited for what seemed like forever. Twiddling my thumbs and pretending I was reading the poster aside me.

Then suddenly "ah its here!" She said.

Oh god, hold on tracey... I thought.

Then she started to mumble, words I couldn't quite make out as she read the letter that had been passed on to the GPs. Now, the doctor I saw this day was not an paediatrician, she was in fact a gynaecologist... talk about complete different end of the spectrum! So she read out what she could understand of the letter.

Then all of a sudden she said something I understood, but was unsure I heard correctly or wish I didn't hear clearly.

"Presenting as a mass on the brain, delayed, appointment to be sent"

She turned and looked and me and simply stated as calm as possible but with an urgency to her tone "you MUST go speak to that Dr as soon as possible".

I said my goodbyes and thank yous, got up, turned to the door and headed to the waiting room where Dan had been waiting for me. At this point I didn't drive and he was basically my taxi. I just looked at him, then walked straight passed towards the exit. Finding my way to outside I started to sob, like really, really sob. I bloody knew it, I knew something wasn't right.

Through tears I started filling Dan in with what was said, he genuinely thought I was pregnant and couldn't understand why I was so upset, we'd manage he said! Wow, how I wish that had been the case but no. Our daughter had a mass or something on her brain and no one had contacted us to tell us. We had to find out this way.

We headed back home, shocked and not knowing where to even begin.

■■

Once home I broke the news to my mam who had been babysitting, there was even more tears. In agreement she would watch them longer while we figured out what was going on.

Dan tried to call the Dr who had arranged the appointment, we got no answer. We tried contacting the reception desk, no answer. We were beginning to change from upset and devastated to frustrated and angry.

"Thats it! We are going there and not moving until someone tells us what the hell is going on" Dan wasn't waiting anymore, why should we? We had waited almost three weeks as it was and we were no further forward. We had to know, we needed to know, and it had to be now.

There we were, just me and dan sat in the waiting room. The receptionist was lovely, understood our frustrations and told us she would make him aware that we were there and needed to speak to him as soon as possible.
We shuffled into the room and took a seat, the angry, frustrated parents we had been an hour beforehand had gone. There was just us, anxiously on edge awaiting to hear the fate of our daughter. Awaiting for someone to tell us who she is, not knowing at the time that, knowing or not knowing didn't actually matter. Delilah is Delilah.

"Im sorry Mr and Mrs Huggins, I had intended on contacting you sooner but you are new to our practice and it can run a little slow...

I don't care I thought, just hurry up...

"Your daughter has what we call delayed myelination, to put it simply myelin is the insulation which surrounds the nerve fibres in the brain which enables the messages to travel from one part of the brain to another smoothly and easily and if it isn't thick enough the messages don't get to their destination as easily and sometimes the messages may get lost along the way. We continue to grow myelin up to the age of 35...."

He spoke continuously for a while after that, barely taking a breath as if to almost quickly say it and then its done.

The only things I can specifically remember being said in that room are these...

'Delayed myelination and Unsure of life expectancy'

"Will pass you onto a doctor that REALLY knows her stuff, she will be in touch".

And that was that.

I heard every single word he had said, but didn't hear a thing. I saw his mouth moving, but didn't understand a word he had said. My brain was foggy, I didn't know what to say or whether to actually say anything. Do I cry? Or am I being silly? Did he really say all that? Am I over exaggerating? Can I remember what he said until I get to our car and google it? We were sent on our way.

There was simply no words I could physically think of. Is she ok? What does this mean? Were we really just about to become one of those families? How were we going to cope? How do I care for her? I was now on high alert.

Why on earth did this doctor allow us to leave with our baby without a clue of how to look after her? It felt as if I was 16 again taking home my baby without a clue of what I had gotten myself into.

That day was the first day that myself and Dan had drove

home in silence. That was the first of many.

■■

Following that initial first appointment so much happened quickly. Dan took the decision to leave his job, which left us with no option to claim benefits. We hadn't been claiming very long when they decided to cut them again, citing that Dans reasoning for leaving work wasn't a good enough excuse. Well, they were wrong. So very wrong, and we actually gained a lot of support.

Not only was our life slowly turning upside down, we had to re-home our beautiful Labrador Marley. Marley was a beautiful dog that had been by my side throughout my pregnancy carefully keeping an eye on me when Dan was at work. Although we had him for three years and he was very dear to us, he was still a little sod. He had flooded our home twice while trying to escape as we weren't in, we were at hospital. The attention he was used to, he wasn't getting anymore. The guilt of being a 'bad dog mam' forced me to look for a new home for him, so that he could be better looked after. He went to a wonderful family who were looking to have him trained for their deaf daughter. This filled my heart with joy, he would never be alone again.

Since then we have had numerous hospital appointments, hospital stays and travelled frequently to Great Ormond St hospital in the hopes of finding a diagnosis. Delilahs genes are now apart of the DDD study and have been since 2014 all in the hopes of getting some answers.

Diagnosis used to be so important to us, we lived and breathed hospital appointments, calls and test results in the hopes of discovering what on earth was happening to order daughter. Not only what was 'wrong' with her, but what her future would look like.

We now know, there is nothing 'wrong' with Delilah. Has she got complications? Yes. Does she have additional needs? Yes. Does it make us, as a family love her any less? Hell no.

We stopped living for a diagnosis once all of the blood specimens that were sent abroad and other places came back negative. When all the MRIs, ECGs, cat scans, lumbar punctures all came up with nothing. Delilah once had a skin and muscle sample taken in GOSH, they took a sample, did loads of technical stuff with it and grew her skin in a laboratory... like how cool is that! Down side? Her skin grew normal. Her skin is far from normal, like soo far from normal...

All of this is, is all of the reasons why we stopped waiting on bated breath for a diagnosis. Why we choose to learn our child, work on what we knew and decided to just deal with each day as it comes. We don't know the future, even with a diagnosis we couldn't know the future anyway's. We know what we know, we know Delilah and that's all we really need in this moment.

■■

Dear Delilah,

How very unique you are...

Delilah has numerous little diagnoses but no overall diagnosis. She is a unique complicated soul, but one that is very determined. To help you understand Delilah a little more I have put below, everything we do know so far-

Nystagmus - Nystagmus is a rhythmical, repetitive and involuntary movement of the eyes. It is usually from side to side, but sometimes up and down or in a circular motion. Both eyes can move together or independently of each other. A person with nystagmus has no control over this movement of the eyes.

AKA - Delilah has shaky eyes, they move side to side and up and down. Normally a nystagmus goes one way or the other, but not Delilah, oh no, hers goes both = unique.

Ichthyosis - Ichthyosis is a term used for a group of conditions that affect the skin, making it rough and scaly. The name comes from the Greek for 'fish' as sometimes the skin may look a little bit like fish scales. Normal skin is continuously shed and re-grown to form an effective barrier against infection and other damage. In ichthyosis, this mechanism does not work properly, so the skin does not shed properly, so builds up as thick, rough areas. How much of the body is affected varies depending on the particular type of ichthyosis.

Simply, Delilah has skin that is incredibly thick, tough, and shed's a lot. You cannot wear black in this house without there being a dusting of skin all over you by the time you leave our home. Delilahs skin can make her very hot, dehydrated and is incredibly itchy. You can often hear me bellowing, "Stop scratching!" Or "i'm gonna knack you if you don't stop scratching!"... to which Delilah obviously responds "but i'm itchy!". So yea, another unique trait of hers is that after testing her skin for ichthyosis, it came back negative. Go figure!

Global Developmental Delay & Autism spectrum disorder - Global developmental delay is an umbrella term used when children are significantly delayed in their cognitive and physical development. It can be diagnosed when a child is delayed in one or more milestones, categorised into motor skills, speech, cognitive skills, and social and emotional development. There is usually a specific condition which causes this delay, such as Fragile X syndrome or other

chromosomal abnormalities. However, it is sometimes difficult to identify this underlying condition.
Autism spectrum disorder (ASD) is a complex developmental condition that involves persistent challenges in social interaction, speech and nonverbal communication, and restricted/repetitive behaviors. The effects of ASD and the severity of symptoms are different in each person.

ASD is usually first diagnosed in childhood with many of the most-obvious signs presenting around 2-3 years old, but some children with autism develop normally until toddlerhood when they stop acquiring or lose previously gained skills. According to the CDC, one in 59 children is estimated to have autism. Autism spectrum disorder is also three to four times more common in boys than in girls, and many girls with ASD exhibit less obvious signs compared to boys. Autism is a lifelong condition. However, many children diagnosed with ASD go on to live independent, productive, and fulfilling lives. The information here focuses primarily on children and adolescents.

Delilah has both a GDD diagnosis and a ASD diagnosis. Both of which are very apparent but don't greatly impact Delilahs life at the moment. Don't get me wrong, some days are worse than others but overall, Delilah is a happy chatty child who knows her own mind. Now to me, that is a strength not a weakness. Is she behind other children her age? Yes. But life isn't a race or a competition... it is a path that everyone takes at their own pace. Delilah is also obsessed with red crips and her iPad, this is how she regulates and we can never be without red crisps.

*Movement disorder - *still under investigation* Dystonia is the name for uncontrolled and sometimes painful muscle movements (spasms). It's usually a lifelong problem, but treatment can help relieve the symptoms.*

As you can see i've added under investigation here as to be honest, we aren't entirely sure... it could be dystonia, it could be Ataxia, or it could be none of the above. All we know is she is constantly shaking and her arms, legs etc all spasm regularly. This can be horrendous on days where she is tired and can quite often hurt herself through it. It is probably one of the most frustrating additional needs for Delilah.

Next! Sorry... this list could go on forever and in fact i'm not sure what else I could really write and divulge that would make you see Delilah in all her unique glory... so instead I shall say this.

My daughter isn't a project, to be tested on and poked and prodded. She is wonderful, funny and unique. She cannot be fixed, mended or have some sort of magic spell put upon her.

Would I take it all away if I could? I'm not sure, could you swear i'd still have the same little sassy pants afterwards if I said yes?

I am guilty of once saying that good old "if I could take it all away...." But in fact in our very specific case I'm not sure. I would love her to have an even better life, but I couldn't change HER. Her disability doesn't make her Delilah.

She is unable to do things as there is lack of access, here where we are. Her wheelchair isn't the problem, access, funding and inclusion is. The sooner this is resolved the more we could offer her. I have no doubt about it.

Delilah has had four or five major surgeries on her hips. Delilah was at the risk of hip dysplasia and we were told it is better to operate when she is younger so she would forget all about it and also heal quicker. It actually hasn't made any difference to her life. She still isn't able to weight bear, stand or sit unaided most of the time. She is no less uncomfortable than she was, so all in all it feels like it was pretty pointless... but that is not to say it was exactly.

■■

Hospital stays are something we tend to also get used to. I wrote a blog about this a little while ago which I feel best sums up the experience of having to stay in hospital with your child.

In That Room, Bottom to the left...

I cannot begin to imagine how many times we have been on that children's ward in that room, all the way to the bottom and on the left. It is known as Delilah's room to Delilah, family and some of the nurses.

It is hard to describe to anyone who doesn't really 'get it' what it is like to be in that room. That room with the farm animals and vinyl stickers that try and brighten the room, but instead make every parent just want to pull that creased edge after staring at it for days on end. From the buzzing of someone at the ward entrance, to the machines beeping, to hearing room such and such's child is upset and distressed or in room etc where their child is happy to go home and wants to play loudly. The discussions you overhear via the nurses about how they are heading home after their shift, that they have plans and a life outside.

The staring and the car park for hours on end, watching people visiting loved ones, seeing people arguing over spaces and ambulances attend to calls. The taste of your first and 16th cup of hospital tea, awaiting visitors just so you can grab a 'proper' one from the cafe and stretch your legs, you take the stairs in order to be a little longer and have a little longer to think. The constant time checks even though you know you're not getting home anytime soon. The constant WhatsApp, messenger and text checks you do to keep people informed, even though you'd rather they left you alone. The posting it on Facebook - not for attention, but for support because your own support network is missing (I see you and understand). The paying for tv you will never watch but will need back ground noise. The magazines you buy but never read and crosswords you intend to fill in but you never do.

The moment the 6th doctor enters the room and asks you to repeat everything you have said to the five before him. The not-so-easy way of describing what is going on when in reality you have no.fucking.clue. BUT you're mam, you know your child inside and out so you must know. The not so easy conversation when your child is undiagnosed and it just sounds like you're reading some sort of list of symptoms from a pamphlet. The little jokes the doctors make to make you feel comfortable, when in reality you're either wishing they'd shut up or you're grateful to have someone to speak to. The endless nurse visits checking temps, and stats to keep an eye on your child all through the day and night... you've not slept for a week. They call throughout the night and you're scared to sleep, do I sleep but what if something happens? What if she gets uncomfortable and wakes up scared? OR what if you fall asleep and the nurse hears you snore or sees you salivate all over the pillow... a trivial concern but a thought and worry non the less.

The want to go home to see your other children, to rest, take a bath and have a good meal...But the guilt that follows and makes you persevere just a few more hours, days or weeks. That slight bit of fresh air you get from the windows that have the safety catches when the rooms are way too hot. The not wanting to be a bother or an inconvenience and finally asking the nurses to point out where the parents kitchen is and sneaking back a luke warm cuppa to your room when it strictly specifies NO HOT DRINKS - luckily they are never hot.

The waiting for your child to have procedure, the long wait for them to come back... the hiccups in-between and after, that *can fill the room in an instant with staff. This is where you jump into mam mode and know EXACTLY WHAT TO DO, although you've never been trained. The shock white faces of visitors who never expected to see your child in that state, they didn't expect to see blood or you jump into action like part of the team. 'This is my reality' you think to yourself as they shuffle out of the room scared.*

It's the friends and family that you grow distant from, because they don't understand. They don't see it, they hear it but they don't 'get it' and why would they? No-one will ever know until it's them. They may see it once in a while, see you there in the chair, in that room watching your child's chest rise and fall with every breath. They will see it, like, actually see it in your eyes, they will feel the atmosphere in the room drop when you stop talking as you're too tired to keep up the conversation and they, well they don't know what to say. The loneliness, the sadness, the bewilderment, exhaustion and the fight you have in you. Then they will walk away, and everything will go back to as it was, but you won't forget that day, week or weeks sat in that room, it will become number whatever out of however many times that you have been in that room, to the bottom on the left.

I don't hate hospital stays at all. Weirdly, when that moments strikes I have a feeling of relief quite often... because right then, in that moment? I have NOWHERE else I need to be. I don't HAVE to answer calls and emails. I don't have to fight a cause, write a list or consider my next step, I am following hers. All I need to do and the only place I need to be is here, in this chair.

And it never changes, each time is the same as the last and each time that follows. It starts to feel like a second home, a peaceful calm can come over you, like a realisation that this is life. Some people have hotel stays and holidays, you, you have this. Luke warm cuppas, magazines unread and all the people watching you. In this room bottom, to the left. Delilahs room.

Delilah's Views On...
Being Unique

Hey beautiful, how do you feel about being special and unique?
Good, because I am more unique than other people.

What do you think it means to be special?
Erm, it means to be loving and kind.

What do you what to be when you are older?
A vet, because I love animals, especially with ALL of these around. (We have two dogs, a hamster and 6 fish...)

Do you think being special will help you do that?
I don't know because if you're in a wheelchair you may be a bit lower than the bed you help pets on.

How do you feel when you're with your friends that aren't special?
It feels kinda good but if they really wanna be special I would give them something to make them special.

What do you think makes you special?
Well my hips are not like other peoples because they need surgery all the time and my skin. My skin is special because I was born with it.

Chapter 3

DO YOU COME HERE OFTEN?

Mummy groups, appointments and tears...

So, here we were. With our little bundle of joy and confusion, not a clue what we are doing or where we were going next. We needed a hand, we needed support and we didn't know what we were looking for.

Our first introduction to the SEND world was a lovely specialist health visitor called Diane. Diane had been referred to us by our very lovely health visitor, Julie. Julie was amazing throughout, she never doubted my fears and encouraged me to have Delilah checked over. For a health visitor, we felt as if she had went above and beyond for us. Giving Julie up was so hard but we were reassured Diane knew her stuff when it came to special needs support. Diane would be our new point of call, a go to and someone who was there to support us as a family, not just with Delilah. We were very lucky in this moment to have Diane as i'm not sure what we would have done if we didn't.

Once Diane had stepped in our lives seemed to have been turned upside down. To be clear, Diane was not the cause haha! We were all of a sudden meeting someone new every other day, or week from all different services. Within a couple of weeks we had a community nurse, a portage team and had already met a specialist in eye movement. We went from cleaning, school runs and Dan working to being if we were in the house we had visitors and if we were out of the house we had appointments.

Everything was a blur, trying to remember names were difficult and which team they had belonged to even harder. I quite often asked "annd who are you again?", fortunately no-one was ever offended, I think they could see we were struggling and plus, unlike us, they had all been in this situation before.

■■

Our portage support at the time was the very lovely Elizabeth. Portage was such a shock to us and we really didn't have a clue what to expect. I had been to messy play groups when my older two children had been younger and thought it obviously must be something like that...

Portage turned out to be THE best free therapy I had ever received. Elizabeth was wonderful and eccentric, we had never met someone so positive and supportive before. She was who we needed in that very moment. There was no doom and gloom, just fun, songs and play. She had all the time in the world for us and I will never forget the feeling of calm she brought our home even though she was so lively.

*If you have ever had a portage session and have NOT heard the song 'what's in the box' please raise your hand... good that's everyone then! I genuinely can't hear anyone ask "what's in that box?" Without singing 'Delilah Huggins' in my head afterwards. - It's a thing honest, i'm not weird. *

Within a few weeks of visits Elizabeth had asked if we had looked into charities such as Tabitha's toys to help with sensory lights and play toys to stimulate Delilah when she was alert, so we reached out and gained some wonderful friends through it. She also asked if we had sought to claim DLA etc and encouraged me to request the forms and that she would sit with us and fill them out "no, no I said, we will be fine!"... yea, we weren't.

Following all the home appointments, the meeting new people and professionals, came the parent groups. Our local group, ran by a group of community nurses, physios and occupational therapists, was designed in order to make us, feel a little reassured about asking questions in a comfortable setting. We were invited along by our community nurses team. The group was called CYGNETS. There was soft-play, sandwiches, tea and coffee and awkward silences between parents.

This was the first time I had ever been to a parent group of this type before. Delilah was around 8 months old and I didn't have a clue still, to what was going on. By the looks of it, not many others did either. We all kind of sat there silently, waiting for someone to speak and to make conversation. It was painful.

What is Portage?

Portage is a home-visiting educational service for pre-school children with SEND and their families.

Portage aims to:

- To work with families to help them develop a quality of life and experience, for themselves and their young children, in which they can learn together, play together, participate and be included in their community in their own right.

- To play a part in minimising the disabling barriers that confront young children and their families.

- To support the national and local development of inclusive services for children.

Who can get portage?

Portage is available to you if you have a young child with additional needs, including with a learning disability.

It is traditionally available to certain disabled children until the age of five.

What happens when you receive portage

If you are eligible for portage, here's what will happen:

A portage worker will visit you and together you'll identify and agree new skills that you want your child to develop. This usually happens on a weekly basis.

The portage worker will then create a plan of techniques and what needs to happen to teach your child these skills.

You'll then follow the plan, practice the techniques at home and the portage worker will track your progress each visit.

How to receive portage visits

Most portage services have criteria to determine who is eligible to receive them. These criteria will vary from area to area.

Not every local area has a portage service. To see if you have portage services in your area, visit the National Portage Association website which has details of all registered portage services and who to contact.

You can also view your council's Local Offer of support, which should have details of a portage service if there is one in your local area.

Cygnet – a baby swan...

Parent groups were not my thing at this time. I tried and persevered because I so wanted to reach out to someone and ramble. I wanted someone to say it's ok, i've been there and done this before. Things will calm down soon, you will get in the swing of it and you won't feel as if you're drowning. Instead I got small talk with a few mums who I know will have all felt the same as me, but we didn't broach the subject... instead we discussed trivial things and stayed silent.

Then there was those 'other' parents. The ones who (this seems judgmental but hold on) that were out for whatever they can get. They discussed applying for funding for iPads, tv's and all sorts. How they took whatever they could, it was like a *excuse my French* pissing contest to which of their children were more in need, more poorly and had more professionals. These were not my type of people and this wasn't where I needed to be right now. My head wasn't in it, I was still learning. So we left and never went back. The few mams I did speak to, I saw in passing over years and still see now and again.

Those parents that I didn't get along with, I can now understand why they were the way they were. I can understand their frustrations of fighting for whatever their child needed and taking what they could, when they could, as otherwise your child would probably get nothing. It's a weird life with very little supportive support, I hope that makes sense? There is a lot of services designed to support parents/carer but not a lot of the services can cater for everyone. It comes down to that good old saying of 'you can bring a horse to water but you can't make it drink' so you can't cater if you don't know what people need. Must be very frustrating.

■■

So, my home was filling with people I didn't know, all telling me things I knew nothing about and I felt isolated from everyone I did know. This moment in time was not fun. It was hard. It was really hard to not feel as if we were alone, I know, sounds strange since I have just wrote that we never caught a break but this was a feeling that would never leave and would one day turn into our reality. Only Dan and I truly know how we felt in that moment, it was our lives that had been turned upside down and shuck like a cocktail shaker. Delilah on the other hand? Had no idea. She didn't care, she has always been very happy, smiley and inquisitive. She slept well, fed well-ish and adored the attention given to her on a daily basis. She took every test they could throw at her, every blood sample, MRI, exploratory surgery and medications they would expect her to take. We had very few tears, well from her anyways...

Me on the other hand? I didn't cope so well. This was MY baby they were poking and prodding. Every time they requested to see her, run tests etc I would nod along. I would allow them to try and discover what it was that created my daughter this way. I didn't know better, so I nodded along not realising that the word no was actually a choice. I think only cared about a diagnosis at that time because I was expected to, but in reality I didn't. I had carried her, I gave birth to her, I was there through it all and it didn't matter because she was mine and I loved her regardless of her 'extras'.

Guilt

Mam guilt is one of those things as a parent you just get used to. You have no choice, you can live with it or fight against it, but either way it won't budge. Sometimes, it will be overwhelming and sometimes it will be a flashing feeling or thought.

After discovering Delilah had numerous additional needs I had instantly started to blame myself. I second guessed everything I had done, everything I had eaten and started to scrutinise myself over and over. In reality, I had never ate soo well during a pregnancy, I never ate sweets too much or fatty foods. I stayed away from the foods on the no go list and Dan watched my every move. He did any heavy lifting, made me rest and took great care of me, especially on those days where I could feel there was something wrong. He would come home, take me to be checked over and make me feel reassured. He had done so much for me, so to me, it MUST have been my fault because I carried her, I was in control for nine months.

So here I was, devastated. Not at all because of her, but because of me. I felt as if I had let her down, as if it was me that was the issue. Overtime, I learnt a lot about the guilt and how to deal with it. I learnt quite simply that Delilah would have always been Delilah, regardless of what I did whilst pregnant. It's just what happens when two people with the same exact broken genes meet and fall in love (barf)... but she is amazing to us, even when she is extra talky ha!

Then, there is the guilt I carried (and still do) of my other children. They have and will continue to miss out on soo much. They didn't see mam and dad so much anymore. They were dropped off to school and picked up by zombies who were sleep exhausted. We changed over night almost, we weren't happy go lucky looking for our next adventure anymore. We were a constant bag of worry and they were too young to understand. We never explained anything to them properly until they reached an older age. Instead we just explained that Delilah is special, will always be different to them and that she will need extra help. She will need mammy and daddy more than them but it doesn't mean they aren't loved. We love them all, equally.

Grief

Oh this is a hard part, it is hard to explain and hard to discuss openly even more so. Guilt is an overwhelming emotion that one day hits you in the face without warning.

Right now you either don't know why you feel the way you feel or you may know exactly how you feel but feel like no one else is talking about it. Well, i'm here to talk about it with you. Grief is something that is unexpected when you learn your child has additional needs. It can hit you out of nowhere and not leave, or it can come and go, always lingering in the background. Either way, it's ok to say it out loud. This is not what you signed up for.

Being pregnant all those years ago I knew that there was something not 'right,' my body constantly told me. I had aches and pains, I had moments where it would feel like she wasn't moving much and like I could go into labour at any moment. I consistently roped Dan into taking me to hospital each time for a check-up and each time being told "she's fine, juicy size but fine". Turns out, my motherly instinct was constantly poking me to alert me of something, something wasn't 'right'.

Having a confirmation of my feelings was horrendous. At this time I was lost. Completely and utterly lost. I was spending more time with my daughter in the presence of professionals, than family and friends. I was angry and upset… these feelings made me feel guilty. I couldn't put my finger on it either, until one day a nurse who offered us respite (I never left the house, I couldn't leave her) had told me I needed to grieve. To give into the grief and I will start to feel better.

Grieve? Why on earth would I grieve? Delilah is here... alive and kicking, I can see her beside me. Why would I grieve?

Here is why I would grieve... I would grieve because this is not the life I envisioned, for her us or our family. I saw her clear as day running wild, playing in the park, climbing the stairs and getting wrong. I saw her acting herself and being told 'no' just for Dan to give in and give her it anyway. I saw it all but that's not what we are experiencing. We had swapped the life I promised myself, my husband even, for something completely out of our comfort zone. I wasn't one of those parents, that I watched on shows, that my heart bled for. I wasn't strong enough to be.

But we didn't get the choice. This was our new path. So I grieved, I felt all of the stages of grief. From shock and anger, bargaining to depression. We went through the full cycle. The last stage we haven't quite got to yet, Acceptance. I will come back to that one later.

Let yourself grieve. Give yourself that time and don't feel guilty for it. It's a natural instinct that occurs, a sadness but it is ok. It is normal.

Isolation

Not everyones story will be the same. Not everyone will feel guilt or grief. Some people are far more resilient than others, some struggle through gritted teeth and some bare all. I have been all three at some point in my life. Not everyone will feel isolated...

Isolation came for me well before the pandemic did, I always say that us SEND parents were in a pandemic before pandemics were 'cool'. We have been in this state for the whole of the lifespan of our children, the hand washing, the caution, the distancing ourselves from people who have viral infections, the not being able to see friends and family and lastly, the thing that people seemed to struggle with the most, the need to rely on people who either A, didn't know what they were doing as they'd never seen it before and B, relying on doctors and professionals to tell us what our next turn is.

From the very moment we discovered that Delilah wasn't going to follow the natural 'normal order' of baby, toddler or child stages, I began to feel people pull away. My friends pulled away, they didn't know what to say, whether they'd upset me by getting something wrong and they didn't want to celebrate their children milestones in front of me incase they upset me.

They did upset me, i'll be honest. My child should have also been doing those things, saying that and reaching that milestone.

Friends became distant and now, nine years on have dwindled down to social media acquaintances, which is difficult at times. If their children are the same age as Delilah and achieving huge things etc I will like their posts, congratulate them in person if I pass and make a fuss. Where Delilahs achievements are much smaller and greater to us, and they don't understand. So I stop sharing at times. We grow either further apart. Even other parent carers can also become great friends that you grow distant from. You then both have busy lives, time that is precious and the inability to keep up a conversation via text at the risk of their being a drama around you that you may miss.

Family, I have a large family, like, you're only ever a stones throw from a Bates (maiden name) up here in Sunderland. I have four sisters and a brother. I live next door to my parents (which comes in handy) and used to have a close relationship with them all. Then I didn't.

Family is a funny old thing, it is a necessary need to make sure everyone is invited and that everyone is ok. It's difficult. Not everyone is the same, not everyone has the same views and beliefs and not everyone sees eye to eye... then add having five girls and one boy.

Growing up we were always close, we used to paint the town red together, have get togethers at the

weekends where then men would play darts and the women would socialise and the kids would run amok until they dropped and slept. We had a good support bubble, we were always together.

When I had Delilah, I changed. I was done with weekend drinks and late nights. I was done with having to socialise and explain why I can't attend playgroups etc and I pulled myself away. I couldn't explain it well enough and they couldn't quite understand. Birthday parties would come and go and we missed almost all of them. We hated soft-play, kids would climb or tumble over Delilah, she would get frustrated and my heart would break for her. We didn't go to discos as Delilah hated loud noises and busy areas. We would just be at home, missing it all, guttered while Delilah played on the floor with her toys, happily.

My family didn't understand, they thought I was making excuses, that I didn't want to attend and I can understand why they thought that. We made 100s of excuses, to save not only Delilahs upset but our own. Because of this, communication broke down and I never really explained the full extent of it. It's hard for the outside looking in to really understand when you're pretending to have all your shit together.

So, I isolated myself. I hid away when I could have been socialising, I pulled myself away from everyone. I didn't really understand at the time but I was upset, angry, frustrated, stressed and lost. I was completely lost and I don't think in that moment anyone could have helped. The only person that could help, was me, and I didn't/couldn't.

———

Find Your Tribe

Find your tribe, you have probably already seen this somewhere or someone may have already given you this advice. Finding your tribe doesn't necessarily mean those with children who also have additional needs, it could be old friends, new friends, work friends or school mam friends. But find your tribe.

Your tribe will consist of those friends that hold back judgement (to your face any ways) who know when to step up and not give you the softly, softly approach. The friends that will show up when you ask them not to, will see you slipping and pull you back up. The friends that will send you a text, a WhatsApp or a gif to remind you they are there... just waiting for you when you are ready to talk.

I didn't find my tribe till much later on, I found my tribe within the SEND sector and outside of it. I have very few close friends (this happens with age right? And the unnecessary need for bullshit, right?). I have a few friends within the SEND world who are there to discuss the hardships, funny bits and stressful bits of our SEND world. We put the world to rights and love a good rant over coffee and cake (tea for me).

Then there is my non-SEND mam friends, who are in awe of me but also know I am a completely utter mess. We will either arrange to go to the gym, pub and theatre together and they know i'll probably not get there but don't make me feel bad about it. These friends will invite me to cafes when i've been a bit quiet so we can eat cheese toasties, strawberry tarts and people watch. I love these days. They don't get my life, but they know me, who I was, who I am now and who I inspire to be one day and encourage me greatly.

If you don't have a tribe, don't worry. Start small, start with online forums, BUT DO NOT OVERWHELM YOURSELF. Everyones story is different, you may not resonate with everyone, and not everyone will be your cup of tea. If you add every support group for each condition you will start to focus on the negatives, look for the positives, if certain groups start to upset you, remove yourself. You have enough on your plate. Then, if you feel up to it, go along to parent carer coffee groups, meet new people, some you will dislike, some you will resonate with and some you will just 'get' one another. You both maybe strong or fragile, both may have common interests away from the children. Or maybe, you'll like no one but enjoy going anyway to listen, to take in everyones opinions and thoughts.

Whatever you do, do what is best for you. You don't NEED a tribe, but trust me when I say, having one is a bloody god send at times.

This is my illustration of what I received and what I actually wish I got.

Chapter 4

WORKING HARD & HARDLY WORKING

Giving up jobs, finding our way, a touch of anxiety with a bow on top...

Dan worked really hard from the day he left school. He was a computer technician at a sixth form college about half an hour away from our home. He has numerous qualifications that I don't understand and can fix everything technological. Things that I break, to be honest.

When Delilah started to spend more time in hospital, appointments and all, it was very scary. It was a time where neither of us could have done it alone, everything we did, we did together and that's how it was. Dan would put in numerous holiday days, would have to dash home or call in saying he would be late. At the time his workplace was also going through a big transition with staffing, as schools always do, everything was turned upside down. They needed him, but so did we.

After a few very long tiring months of trying to juggle Dan

was called into work to see his boss. Dan was really struggling between the work and home life balance and something had to give. That was the exact ultimatum they had given him, if he didn't leave they would have to let him go... bullshit right? I know!

But that was the case and we knew it was coming. I am not a money orientated person, I am definitely a 'can't take it with you!' type of person, which Dan hates with a passion some days, but hey ho! So, I had always told Dan "if it isn't making you happy, then leave, we will find our way and cope with whatever comes. We don't need any extra stress right now"... so that's what he did, he walked away. Something he had once loved, something he had spent a lot of time in but yet never progressed any further had frustrated him and this was the final straw.

■■

We were without a wage, without a plan and without any money. We still had bills, we still had a car to pay for, with the added extra of X amount of car parking charges, meals on the go, cuppas and trying to keep our other children entertained. Never mind the endless nappies, vests and creams we bought 'to try'.

So we had to seek benefits. Now I don't know where they came up with the term 'benefits' but I do feel they really need to hold a consumer meeting and think about renaming them, as there is certainly no 'benefits' in having benefits.

We had no idea what to do so we contacted our local job centre. There is a terrible misconception that everyone who applies for benefits or attends a job centre are 'dole wallers', 'scroungers' or some sort of disgusting lower class. When in reality, it is there to help you get by, whether its short term or long term that is a support that is necessary, without money you can't live, you can't provide meals for your children or necessities. So this is what we had to do.

We spoke to a really, really helpful gentleman who took everything we said into consideration, listened carefully to our fears and reassured us that what we were doing was right and necessary for the situation we were in. Dan had worked every single day from leaving school, literally the day after he left, he went straight into higher education AND work at the same time. This was a massive shift for Dan, he struggled with this so much. Because he struggled, I struggled. I did not know what to do or say to support him, I just did what I could to help us get by.

A man's pride is hard to communicate, they are the lion of the family, they are there to provide, ensure security and protect us all. Men have always been portrayed as the strong one, the man behind mam who holds the home up. The guy who should be working, who shouldn't show emotion or crumble. The stereotypical man. The forgotten parent.

■■

We did everything right, we thought. We weren't asking for anything that we weren't supposed to be entitled to and were simply asking for a hand while we found our way. It is pretty common in parent carers to need to rely on benefits when going through a shift of spending more time at home. The process is long and pretty frustrating to say the least.

By the time we had issued our forms and went through the long process we discovered we were entitled! Surprise, surprise! Now I don't begrudge the system, we are lucky to have it and we should certainly not look down our noses to those that depend on it as everyones situation is different, but... to say we benefited from it would be lies.

Within a short period they turned and changed their decision citing that the reasoning for dan leaving his job wasn't good enough. Oh I am sorry... were you going to come to all of our appointments and hold Delilah down whilst they took blood samples while dan goes back to work mr decision maker? I think not. It would cost the government a hell of a lot more if I asked them to pay for all of the roles we do take on as carers, surely?

Anyways, I digress.

We weren't entitled to anything, so after a few trips to our local job centre with ALL of our paperwork to date in hand, we sat and went through everything and made our case. Once again, we were successful and it was then decided we were instead entitled to income support instead of job seekers allowance.

They cited that Dan would not be expected to rush back to work and would support us for the mean time... funny that?

As if life isn't tough enough at that moment we had to bare our souls and ask for something that although entitled to it, never wanted it. I am not ashamed to say that we lived on benefits for two almost three years before we settled into a new regime, life and started to have new prospects. Both of us.

■■

We started to find our feet, as we were finding our feet we had a great routine. Dan kept me going and we did all of the appointments together BUT I did the majority of the talking. We took everything in our stride and having both of us there, what one of us missed the other heard and picked up on. We were becoming the ultimate team. Within the first year of her little life we had cancelled a christening, rebooked and held it. We had planned a big wedding for summer 2013, cancelled it and rebooked it for the registry office in February 2013... we then forgot about the wedding and started to plan it SEVEN weeks beforehand The size of it didn't matter to us just the initial meaning and the bond between us was what mattered. We moved house, actually we swapped houses with my parents. We moved to the house next door. My parents were looking to downsize and we were looking for more space, Delilah was starting to have A LOT of equipment delivered and we didn't have much room to cater. We were smashing appointments, turning up on time, the travelling, everything. But obviously... not everything goes to plan all the time does it?

■■

It was May bank holiday 2013, we had an appointment at the North East Children's Hospital in the Royal Victoria Infirmary in Newcastle. From our home, it is about a half an hours travel in the car in traffic, which we had expected. It was a 9.30am appointment and traffic would be bad due to work commuters.

Now I do apologise for this bit, but I will be quick and not very graphic where possible.

That morning I didn't feel right. I knew something was lingering but couldn't figure it out. Everyone tried to reassure me it was just nerves, today was a big day, we were meeting Delilahs new neurologist and running through some specific tests in order to hopefully help towards a diagnosis for Delilah. Today was huge. I had to be there, I had to be there for Delilah and to support Dan, and him to support me.

We were stuck in traffic when it hit me, the urge to vomit and 'go' all at once was overwhelming. I got Dan to pull out of traffic and into a side street where there was a pub, that obviously was shut. I was devastated, I started to panic and got scared. This could be one of thee most embarrassing moments of my life and I couldn't cope with what was happening. I jumped back in the car where we went as fast as we could to hospital, where I locked myself in the bathroom and didn't leave. Fortunately, Delilahs room had its own bathroom and in order to not infect anyone else I consistently washed my hands and stayed there.

The Norovirus was EVERYWHERE at this moment in time and the nurses had told me I would have to leave the hospital. Which we expected and had already arranged for me to be picked up to go home. Trust me, I didn't want to be there either but I needed to be. I needed to be there for Dan and Delilah, I needed to go through everyday up until that point with the doctor so he knew exactly what had been going on. I need to be there so that if one of us had forgotten something, the other would remember. We were a team, we worked together and I had to head home.

I was devastated when I got home, I dropped to my knees and sobbed. I felt that I had let her down.

I felt unwell for a few days, a few days turned into a few years...

■■

Turns out, I had traumatised myself that day. The stress of leaving them behind, being unwell and struggling, really had taken its toll on me. Every time I tried to venture out the house I felt unwell, every time I thought about appointments and hospital stays I made myself ill. I tore myself between the idea of not being able to go and feeling the need to have to be there. Some days i'd cave and go, some days I would have to cancel as I physically couldn't manage it. I was my own worst enemy.

I lived like this for a few years, torturing myself, isolating myself further and living within my comfort zone of just me, Dan and the kids. It was hell.

Anxiety is something that everyone has at some point in their lives, whether it's a new job, appointment or taking a leap into the unknown. Those feelings of butterflies in your stomach, a dry throat, a dizzy head and the urge to run. Anxiety is based on fight, flight or freeze. In that moment you have to choose whether you stick it out and stay or whether you leave. Quite often I left, or just didn't get there to start with.

After a very long struggle I headed to the doctors, he prescribed me medication that I chucked in the back of the cupboard and forced myself to attend CBT sessions. Yet, nothing helped. I understood what was wrong with me but couldn't talk my brain out of struggling. It was having none of it. So it got to a point where it felt like it was just me and my anxiety, holding hands in a dark corner.

The thought of leaving the house was strong, but the hours in the house were soul destroying, I needed a hobby. I'm a crafty person at heart, I love to make things cute and pretty. Delilahs equipment up to this point were all black and grey. Drab looking, and unappealing to anyone never mind our daughter. I think the look of the equipment actually scares parent carers more than the job they actually do. Which is such a shame isn't it? So I figured a way to make them more appealing. I started by dressing her callipers, then harness covers and so on. Soon enough I was in the local paper talking about how I was willing to do it for anyone and everyone. Shortly after the requests starting coming in and I started to speaking to more families in a similar situation, while still holding my cards close to my chest.

My crafty-ness got bigger, it got bigger seemingly over night actually. I learnt how to make hair bows and accessories which would take me down a path I never expected. I always wanted to give back to charities and wards that had supported our family and this is how I would do it. Soon enough selling accessories and giving the money to charities became 'my thing'.

Slowly but surely I began running this whole little empire from home. Providing stores and markets with children's accessories and being solely independent. Just Dan and I working away while dealing with every day parent carer stuff.

We did it all from home, without leaving or dealing with anyone, I had dan answering messages and pretending to be me... calling everyone 'hun' 16,000 times as if I was some real housewife of Sunderland, and splashing around smiley faces making it look like i'd lost the plot, but it worked.

We worked, we were working. From this it became a fully fledged legitimate registered earning for us. I was constantly inspired and created lots of new designs. I was doing so well, and created such a great name for myself. I was Tracey, the bow lady. There wasn't nothing I couldn't do, from home.

Then one day, a mum from the cygnets group had reached out to me to buy some of our items. When she came to collect we stood for ages chatting, then again then next time, then we'd chat online. I'd not really seen any of the parents from that group unless it was passing in hospital waiting rooms, giving each other the nod or a quick 'hello, how you guys doing'... nothing in depth, no conversation and we all kind of kept ourselves to ourselves.

Then one day, this mum invited me to a coffee group in the local special needs school her child attended, Delilah on the other hand had been advised to move into a mainstream provision (more on this in the next chapter). So I was never aware of these coffee groups, these meets after school drop off and felt like I was being invited into a whole new world from my little room where I worked any chance I could, and the home where I was mam, carer and wife.

I cancelled. I fell at the first hurdle, I text that morning and cancelled. I couldn't go. I didn't know where it was, who was there, and most importantly, I couldn't leave at the drop of a hat as I would usually if needed as Dan wasn't taking me, I didn't drive and I was being picked up. Fuck. So I cancelled.

Except, she didn't care. She showed up anyway's, feeling guilty I went out and jumped in the car, we chit-chatted all the way, the whole time my stomach in knots, wondering if I could make an excuse and leave and arrange for Dan to collect me. When I got there, I quietly walked into a small room with a few lovely, smiley faces, I was offered a seat and a cuppa. It wasn't so bad... I chatted with the other mams about the trials and tribulations of having a child with additional needs, we laughed about the amount of nappies we changed and the stupid things people said to us. It felt like I belonged there, it felt like these were my people. From that day on I tried to not cancel as much, make myself open to cuppas either at our house or out and about. I started to take my medication and listening to others suggestions. I worked on myself, it wasn't easy AT ALL. I still cancelled now and again but didn't beat myself up about it too much, because at the end of the day what on earth would that achieve? It wasn't always plain sailing, I didn't know how to cope with people, friendships and having this seemed like an extra on my plate that sometimes I couldn't cope with. Sometimes, I wasn't a great friend and I can see that now.

But, since that first coffee group I have packed in my business, as I never stopped working when home, Dan has found a new job he loves and is becoming a manager. I passed my driving test, we have travelled all over for fun and appointments and became independent again. I am in charge of my own life again and it feels so damn good.

Anxiety, things to remember

It is soo easy to be bulldozed with any mental health condition, whether it is anxiety, stress or depression. It is really important to remember to help yourself in which ever way suits you best, as after all it is you whom is struggling.

Things to try and remember,

- *Self Care* - this is something you will have either heard or will hear loads. Make sure you have some form of 'self-care', the thing is most of the time the people instructing you to, has no idea how busy you are. So, from me to you, this is doing whatever you do to have five minutes to yourself. Some people go for long walks, read books, lie in the bath to escape their family or simply hide under the stairs. Whatever tickles your pickle, go for it.
- *Ask for help* - it isn't easy to ask for help or take it when its offered. We tried and cope with everything alone and sometimes we are pretty unrealistic on how much we can cope with. So if someone offers to babysit, accept if you're comfortable, if not then don't. If someone offers to make you a cuppa, take it, if you're struggling, invite someone for a cuppa. There is no shame in struggling and saying so.

- *Medication* - this is such a taboo subject still. I have no idea how or why but it is. It isn't a weakness to take prescribed There is no shame in counselling, dumping all your problems onto a trusted stranger or crying in the bathtub. There is no shame in shouting 'fuck it' and having a tantrum although not advised in public.
- *You are not alone* - I know it feels like you are, but you aren't. It is extremely difficult to reach out that first time, but when you do you will feel soo much better for it. Whether it's going to meet someone for a cuppa, responding to someone on social media or doing a parent support group. At least one of these people will resonate with you. It's not easy to break a facade but when you do, others break theirs too and those that do can become good friends.
- *Mindfulness, meditation and positive thinking* - I will be honest this stuff isn't for me. I was an emo as a teen and calm isn't my nature, but I do know that it is other peoples cup of teat and can be beneficial.
- *Keep moving* - Working out isn't just good for your body, it is great for your mental health. When your body moves it releases happy endorphins and this makes your mood feel better. I am not saying go to the gym and lift 50kilos or to start training for your local 5k but instead go for a walk, short or long. Take in some fresh air and do as much as you're fit to do, do as much as you want to do and do it in your own time.

Chapter 5

WELCOME TO THE SEND WORLD

Thrusted into the world of tumble forms, tantrums, paperwork and bugs...

O h, DLA... the mighty trauma that any parent or carer of a child with additional needs must endure. It's a headache, a heartache and a realisation. A realisation that, as much as we like to think otherwise, this is life now. My child is, in deed, disabled and she will not 'get better'.

Applying for DLA was one of our biggest hurdles we faced, I'm not ashamed to say that we considered ourselves to be 'too proud' to even consider applying originally. We didn't feel as if our circumstances would qualify. Delilah was nine months old when we were told we MUST apply, because we will need that label. Even though we didn't want it, and the thought of it was unbearable, we had to have it in order to gain further support.

Side note - I know, I go off topic a lot! But... how ridiculous is it? How ridiculous that unless you are in receipt of a benefit the likelihood of getting some proper support is very slim.

Anyway, we were advised to apply, I knew what was coming though when filling out that particular form. At nine months old I wasn't really doing anymore, in regards to her care needs than what I would have done for my other two children. I was doing my motherly duty, changing nappies, feeds, playtime, bathing, sleep routines and strolls out and about.

The hefty paperwork hit our doormat one morning and the idea of physically sitting down to fill it out made me exhausted. I didn't know what to expect but I knew it would be a headache and that for all I put into it, we would be unsuccessful.

And that is exactly what happened.

We received a letter within a few weeks that pretty much stated exactly what I had thought... we were not doing anything that you wouldn't do for an average child of that age. "They're right", I said to Dan, and I didn't think about it again.

Shortly after receiving that letter we had an appointment with our wonderful portage therapist, Elizabeth. We loved Elizabeth, me especially. I loved her straight to the point attitude. The fact that she told me exactly what I had to hear, even though I may not have wanted to hear it, I needed to hear it. During the visit I had explained we weren't entitled to DLA and that we had been declined. I didn't expect what would be her response, but it went along the lines of "this is ridiculous! You must appeal, i'm telling you now, that bairn is entitled and if you don't get it, someone who ISN'T entitled will, and I won't have it!"... and who the hell was I to disagree? I knew nowt at this point. So, we got the paperwork out and she went through it with us and explained each question in depth. Explained what I was doing as extra care and making me see where I had become a carer over 'just' mam stuff.

I'll never forget this line...

"You MUST focus on your worst day. So, what do you do in order to care for Delilah on one of her 'bad days'"

And that was that. We sent the forms away, which by the way 'got lost' just for Dan have to fax through each individual sheet after explaining it had been three months since we initially applied and WE DIDN'T EVEN WANT IT... but we had to have the label. A phone call the following day with the same gentleman had told us Delilah was entitled, not just entitled, but entitled to higher rate care.

And that was that, it didn't sink in, we were just pleased our first fight was over.

The day the award letter arrived was horrendous. We had known for a few weeks that she had been awarded, but the letter made it a reality. A reality we were not expecting to ever face. Our daughter was in deed disabled. Someone else had taken the time to read her short life and deem that she will be in the need of A LOT of care in the future. Fuck.

Disability Living Allowance

Overview

Disability Living Allowance (DLA) for children may help with the extra costs of looking after a child who:
is under 16
has difficulties walking or needs much more looking after than a child of the same age who does not have a disability
They will need to meet all the eligibility requirements.

The DLA rate is between £23.70 and £152.15 a week and depends on the level of help the child needs.

DLA rates for children

Disability Living Allowance (DLA) for children is a tax-free benefit made up of 2 components (parts). The child might qualify for one or both components.

How DLA for children is paid

DLA is usually paid every 4 weeks on a Tuesday.
If your payment date is on a bank holiday, you will

usually be paid before the bank holiday. After that you'll continue to get paid as normal.
All benefits, pensions and allowances are paid into your bank, building society or credit union account.

Care Component

Lowest weekly Rate £23.70

Middle weekly Rate £60.00

Highest weekly Rate £89.60

Mobility Component

Lower weekly Rate £23.70

Higher Weekly Rate £62.55

Extra Help

You might qualify for Carer's Allowance if you spend at least 35 hours a week caring for a child who gets the middle or highest care rate of DLA.

All information was correct at the time of writing, for more information please check the .GOV website.

From this moment onwards, everything changed. Equipment came thick and fast and our home became a lot smaller. Space was limited and each individual activity had a different piece of equipment, thankfully lifting her wasn't a problem back then and we were able to get the best out of her when she was sat comfortably.

We had a tumble form for play time, a weirdly comfortable seat for Delilah even though it didn't look it. It was bright blue and made of some sort of hard foam stuff (bit of technical terminology there for ya, you're welcome, haha!) It was fantastic, it gave her a great sitting position to stop her aspirating too much when she ate. It allowed us to play on the floor together comfortably and when she was tired but restless she could sit further back and play with her fibre optics until she drifted off. We loved the tumble form.

Then there was the Bee chair, this was the cutest chair we ever did have, although the most shocking one. It was big, it was bulky and it really drummed it in that this was life now. She looked lost in it at the beginning, she was soo small! Small, fragile and oh so very cute! Our bee chair was delivered the day before her first birthday, so the following day at her party she was able to see everyone from a great height, comfortable and able to celebrate with all the chocolate she could wash her face in, true story! This was her life now and this was the first piece of equipment that showed her disability.

Next came the monkey stander, this was some hefty piece of kit! It didn't look it with its bright monkeys and blue tray, with inset bowl for messy play. It was soo heavy to manoeuvre, and Delilah hated it... that's until she got in it. With her bright pink Pedro boots strapped up tight and all of the straps supporting her, she was stood up tall. She could see the world from her feet and she loved it, once she was in it. Delilah seemed to follow the same pattern of most kids, she DID NOT want to do it, be put in it or get out of it once in it haha! It offered great support and did its job, just like most of this equipment.

Then came Delilahs first ever walking frame... the r82 pony. Oh we had a love/hate relationship with her walker. We loved it as it meant Delilah could walk! Woohoo! Fantastic! Except she hit EVERYTHING, tables, chairs, door frames, furniture and limbs. My shins were constantly bruised off where she would run at me unable to stop just to shout a load of waffle at me then go away again. She loved it, we loved it and we were guttered when she out grew it and moved to a bigger walker that she couldn't use as well. That was the end of her walking, we never did managed to find a suitable walker that wasn't too big and bulky for her little legs so that she would be able to move around freely.

This was just a little introduction to the equipment that would engulf our home. From that moment onwards it was all about bath chairs, accessible cutlery, cups, comfortable seating, hoists, safety bed, changing table and wheelchairs. Oh the wheelchairs...

Equipment Needs

How to access equipment to meet your Childs needs

In order to discover what your child would be entitled to please contact your local authority, community nurse, paediatric team, or physiotherapist in order to be referred to the occupational therapy team. You can self refer but to be honest it can sometimes be better if someone else refers your child.

Children in UK have all medical aids and equipment that is required for health reasons for free. This means any piece of equipment that is not deemed necessarily required in order for your child to meet their care needs but is instead an alternative to one offered for free, you are expected to self fund. In these circumstance your physiotherapy team and occupational team can write supporting letters towards gaining funding for you to self fund using a charity etc.

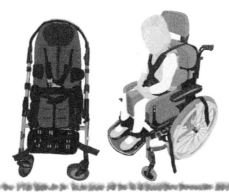

Delilahs first wheelchair was an Ormesa bug stroller. I loved it, easy to manoeuvre, comfortable and pretty cool looking to be honest. Delilah loved to be able to see the world when we were out and about, smiling at everyone and giving everyone a mouthful. For all we loved her bug, I will never forget the first time we took her out.

I was soo excited to take our girl out in her new wheels, it was lilac and black, not overly obvious that it was a wheelchair and we had applied for funding in order to buy the hood and apron that it so desperately needed.

Side note - Again - told you I never stay on topic! Why the heck does things like this never come altogether? I'm not buying a pram, this isn't a fancy accessory, its a necessity. It is mind blowing that they don't think when providing your child a wheelchair in order to physically move that they may get wet, or need shade etc... grr boils my pee... Any way...

So we were off out for the day. I wanted to take Delilah into our local town centre in her new wheels to do a bit of shopping and wandering, as any mum does. Delilah was 15 months old so still quite small and oblivious to the world around her. I think we were in town for a whole twenty minutes, maybe? From the moment we parked, to the moment we got back to the car it had seemed like everyone was breaking their necks to look at her. I think back now that they were probably just trying to figure out whether it was a wheelchair or a pram, either that or just damn rude. Either way it was enough to make me want to leave. I couldn't cope with the amount of people that were either gawping at my daughter OR completely ignorant and pushing into her wheelchair. Had this LOOKED like a wheelchair would they have done the same? Would they have looked then walked on by as she would have been a 'normal looking' disabled child? Either way, it hurt. I did go back, obviously, I just didn't rush back until I had spoke to others in my shoes.

The next time we went out, we went out with our head held high. Since then Delilah has moved up to a 'big girls' wheelchair. It's a shocking pink one and we change the images on her spoke guards often. We give people something to stare at, we are proud of Delilah and Delilah is more than comfortable being in her chair, for now. She's only nine after all.

■■

Throughout this whole period of time, it was just a whole lot of figuring out. Figuring out what worked for Delilah and us as a family, not just Delilahs parents. Although we got it drastically wrong sometimes we were still learning. We are still learning too, that never goes away. There was a whole lot of tantrums, myself and Delilah. Delilah because everything was new, although she knew no different this was all new to her. It was all new to us too, this wasn't a situation we had ever been in before either. This wasn't your average bouncer, pram or car seat. This was a whole other world. This was the world of SEND and we were dropped into it without a parachute. Our home was quiet and calm, and the next day was busy and full. We were never prepared for this, we were never warned, we just had to do what we could and try our best, regardless of our fears.

■■

At this point we had the OT's, the physiotherapists and anyone else you could possibly have. We had moved home in order to gain space and thought that we had all we needed. Yea, you guessed it. We were wrong, we needed more. Our home needed adapting. We needed our floors levelled, our door frames widened and our back door moving. We went from having two windows in our living room, front and back, to having double doors into the garden. We had Delilahs bedroom moved downstairs and hoists fitted in the living room and her 'once dining room but now bedroom'. We had what used to be a good old 'wash house'... I have no idea why it was called this but it was... turned into an en suite shower room and our front garden levelled for access. Not only had our lives turned upside down our home was too. Although a lengthy process it was actually one we welcomed.

We had our home made accessible via the DFG. The disability facilities grant, a grant that enables you to have your home adapted at the cost of your local authority. It is a lot to explain, so I won't but I will add information for you to look into. As not every local authority offers the same services as you may have already discovered by now.

Once completed Delilahs bedroom was downstairs, I absolutely hated it. Like I couldn't hate the idea of something more. Her room was downstairs and ours was upstairs on the far end of the house. We had a monitor but this just wasn't enough, I needed to be closer to her. You may already know what it feels like to leave your child downstairs in their room, but if not it is awful. Going to bed each night and leaving her downstairs sucked, she was only four years old.

The nights that Delilah was unwell meant we slept on our uncomfortable sofa bed in the living room. Soon enough we started spending more nights on there than our actual bed. It was either that or carry her up and down the stairs to our bed, but as she was getting bigger this was just not a possibility anymore. So I took it upon myself to make arrangements to have her moved back upstairs. It was better for us all...

Until it wasn't.

When Delilah started having surgery on her hips as they were at risk of dislocating, we needed her to be comfortable when she was on bed rest. She would have surgery on both hips at different times, so once again the bed came back downstairs. If I remember rightly, it went back up and down again once more before we settled on the fact it would stay downstairs.

These are the struggles that others don't consider. They think the house is adapted with a ramp and widened door and all you have to consider is the redecorating but it isn't. It is the emotional worries and fears of leaving your child downstairs night after night, the waking up during the night to hearing your child choke on vomit and tackling a flight of stairs whilst tired at a great speed. It is all of this and more. It is a huge deal.

And the cost? Doesn't matter. The price to make our home accessible doesn't matter really, because it doesn't take anything away or solve every problem and difficulty.

■■

So how did we alleviate the fears and issues? We haven't. Sorry, I don't have an answer but I will say that this year we had a massive turn around by something that is becoming bigger and better.

Assistive technology.

Delilah had the same routine every night. She would have iPad time to wind down and regulate, then lie on the sofa where me or dad would nurse her off to sleep. Once she drifted off Dan would carry her to bed, she got too heavy for me a while ago. Once in bed we would sneak off to bed and put our cctv camera on that was set up in her room so we could keep an eye on her. Dan was really starting to struggle with the heavy lifting and something needed to change. We had tried everything, every routine you could imagine in order to allow her to drift off in her own bed. She was having on none of it. Until earlier this year we were assigned to a wonderful OT, on a new visit we got to chatting about the exhaustion of bed time etc. I found myself waffling away to her so easily, she was so easy to speak to and so lovely to me and Delilah. Then next day she called me and asked if we wanted to try be apart of a new service they were hoping to offer. All we would need to do is take a few photos and give some feedback, easy peasy, we said yes.

The following day I had a call and arranged a visit with the team lead, he was also lovely and simply asked "what would make your life easier tracey?"...

God where do you start? I actually didn't quite have an answer.

I explained my troubles with having Delilah downstairs, the fears I had and the fact that I can never get downstairs quick enough when she called for us. Then, he had a whole plan in seconds! He had almost fixed my fears! They would fit Alexa shows, link up our devices and enable us to see her and talk to her.

"What else?" He said...

Well, bedtime is hell I said... she won't stay in her bed and we can't watch tv we want to watch, there is no 'us' time anymore. We then had a plan for that, then the hassle of propping her up when people called at the door. Issue after issue he told me how we could not necessarily solve it but make it more manageable.

Delilah now has her whole room linked to her Alexa, from turning lights on and off, opening her blinds and turning on her tv. It's amazing, she can drop in on mam and dad in the living room when feeling scared from being in her room alone on a night.

She now goes to bed, watches tv and then turns it off and goes asleep. It's been a god send for us. I know that this service is new but I am soo keen to see it grow in the future so will support the local authority on this in whichever way they'd like. So keep an eye out if your not north east based for new things coming in your local authority!

Disabilities Facility Grant

The disabilities facilities grant covers adaptions to your home such as widen doors and install ramps. They also can help improve access into other rooms in your home by adding a stair lift or adding new facilities such as a bathroom. The grant also can help with providing a better heating system or adapt heating and lighting controls for accessibility.

A disability facilities grant will not affect any benefits that you are entitled to.

When applying for grants towards adaptions for a disabled child under the age of 18 none of the parent or carers income will be taken into account.

To find out how much you maybe entitled to within the grant, please visit the .Gov website for further information and directions on what to do next.

Chapter 6

FIRST DAY OF SCHOOL

EHCPs not as easy as your ABC's... trust me

O h this chapter is going to be a hard one, not so much emotionally but to explain the mind field of schools, is a tricky one. School, was one thing we got right and terribly wrong all at once. You know that good old saying 'god loves a trier?' Well, just remember that throughout this chapter because it sums it up pretty well.

■■

As I previously explained, Delilah had regular visits from members of our local portage team. The portage team worked well with Delilah and helped her learn her core strengths in fine motor skills, speech and numbers, colours etc. They were brilliant and really brought Delilah on, which was fantastic! Seeing her little face every time one of them visited was a blessing, she loved singing the nursery rhymes and would quite often try to rush them to that bit! She has always been an eager diva!

I never quite realised how crucial their quirky visits were. They were so much more than nursery rhymes and songs, they were crucial in discovering Delilahs next stage. Mainstream or medical provision? The question every SEND parent dreads, you as a parent see your child in a different light... that good old "oh they are mine so you know, i'm biased" really comes into play here. One part of you really wants to highlight all of those wonderful things your child has learnt...

Oh look! She can count to six! She misses out three, but that's ok...

Oh look! She said car! - No Tra, that's just her waffling again...

It is so easy to see the positives.

But then, you feel you need to really highlight the negatives incase they miss the opportunity to be in the right setting. So each time a professional would say, "Oh but she is great at XY & Z" id say, yes but she struggles at AB & C. This wasn't me being negative this was me being fearful that my daughter would be missed. That she would miss where she NEEDED to be because she was being assessed on a hour a weeks visit, some tick boxes and songs.

Planning school was so difficult for so many reasons, it was a complete different experience to the previous two experiences I had faced with my two older children.

For instance, the first two times went like this...

1st time -

- I picked a school

- I signed her up

- I bought her uniform

- We had a visit

- She started school with everyone else, I said goodbye and trusted the staff to care for her, no questions asked.

2nd time -

- He was to go to the same school as his sister

- Was accepted straight away due to this.

- Bought his uniform

- Had a visit

- Started along with everyone else, granted he didn't like it and cried a lot and I sat on kiddies chairs for about two weeks pregnant with Delilah but still, minimal hassle.

Delilah on the other hand, was a much more lengthy process with so many hiccups it was unreal. It was definitely one of the most stressful experience's I had ever been through, I mean i've put up a full room of Ikea furniture before and that was a breeze compared to this...

To start you need to have an idea where you'd like your child to have a placement, view the school, then you need to hold an EHCP meeting and then finally you need check the school is fully prepared to take your child, this includes equipment, staff etc in place ready for the start date.

This bit here? This is where it becomes a mind field, it shouldn't be but it is, I have no Scooby why, but turns out it is just a rite of passage we all must endure.

So what is an EHCP?

An education, health and care (EHC) plan is for children and young people aged up to 25 who need more support than is available through special educational needs support.
EHC plans identify educational, health and social needs and set out the additional support to meet those needs.

AKA a good 40 page document (sometimes) that enlists every requirement that your child may need to support their health care needs and their educational needs whilst in education. This is where you would have things like...

- Support at mealtimes / applying feeding tubes etc

- Medication administered

- Changing and changing facilities

- 1:1 or 2:1 care (how many supporting members of staff your child requires)

- Equipment to be used by your child, seating, computers and stationary

- How often they are changed, if they need creams applying etc how long it will take

- Support out and about in the yard, support in the school

Everything will be minuted and took into consideration, everything will also be costed. I won't go into all of that because quite frankly it can be a bit much to drone on about and I haven't got all day, and i'm guessing, neither do you. Please google it and look into it more...

Side note - again, you know how they say NEVER google anything... I google everything. I don't take it as gospel and not everything is relevant to my situation but I feel I need the general gist of things so I can stay in the loop.

So basically it is pretty vital that you get everything you can think of into the EHCP before it heads off to the SEN to be approved. Once approved your named school will be on the returned draft you will receive. This will mean that quite basically, the school you have named and met etc have agreed that they are able to apply all of the care needs listed by you, your Childs professionals and team in order to start that school. You will then have 14 days to reply if you are not happy with the school choice or need to make any amendments.

The misconception here is that once those 14 days are up and that your child starts the school and hates it and everything may have gone terribly wrong that you are stuck. This is not the case exactly...

Delilah started a local nursery to us, she was deemed 'too clever' to go to the local special needs provision and to be honest although I was slightly upset and nervous about her attending a mainstream school I thought if anything it may encourage her to keep developing. Delilah had been doing so well with portage and we thought she would be great once in nursery.

We had the whole meeting process, we had her EHC plan down, we didn't have as much in it back then as we do now mind but we had a good start. Delilah had a lovely 1:1 that made dropping her off so easy, plus she was only ever there half a day! Also we just lived around the corner so it never felt like I was abandoning her. Delilah also knew this routine, kinda, she got up she got ready then she played and sang songs, we had this down to an art. It was daunting dropping her off in the beginning but I soon got used to it, just as I did twice before.

Nursery was a breeze. We smashed it. Delilah smashed it.

Then, then came the next step. Reception and 'proper' school. This bit was soo much harder. Once again, we went local, a mainstream school that had never had a student like Delilah before. Now, this should have been an insight in what was to come but nope, not to me and Dan, we thought this will be fab! Delilahs made friends in nursery, they will continue on with her and in the process we can help the school learn the art of our child. There is only going to be her in this school with this level of needs so she will get enough attention, she won't be lost in the masses.

I don't think I am the first SEND parent to ever worry about sending their child into school with the fear of them being lost amongst the able bodied children or not getting the care and attention that I had given her. I needed someone to take over mam, to do everything I do and I will be able to sleep at night knowing Delilah was well looked after.

Delilah didn't adjust as well at her mainstream school as we would have liked, she was scared and so were we.

First day of school was horrendous, I looked around at everyone taking their kids to school, walk up to the teacher, hand their child over and walk away. I was soo jealous. Not one person in that school yard could have understood how it felt to be in our shoes, unlike those parents, I had to have two meetings, two break downs of communication, a meeting about equipment that lead to an argument with the head teacher and me declaring I was never taking Delilah to that school. Yet, here I was sat in the car awaiting it to get a bit quieter to take Delilah in, it was just too busy to go in yet.

We had already met Delilahs new 1:1, we instantly loved her, she was our cup of tea, she was down to earth, great with Delilah and they got on like a house on fire. Granted, Delilah and both Danielle (she doesn't mind me naming her, we are still in touch) were nervous in each others company at first. Delilah wasn't used to someone having a no excuses attitude with her and Danielle never had a child like Delilah to care for before, but she was so keen to learn, not just learn but take over everything I did plus extra where she could. Reception was great, she did well. A few learning curves, but that was to be expected...

Year 1 onwards was when it became more difficult.

■■

When a child moves into year 1, school days become more structured. Their work feels soo hard to them and the days spent playing, that they were so very used to, become a lot less. It can be a huge shift for some kids and they struggle to cope with the new routine.

Delilah followed onto year 1 along with her wonderful 1:1 from reception. Delilah was 1:1 throughout her days, but then 2:1 during any changes, physio sessions and mealtimes. These were important as these are the moments where Delilah struggles the most. This was very important to have nailed down, as her mam I am used to juggling a few things at once but at school she needed the full attention throughout these moments.

Delilah struggled throughout year one and two. Not only did she struggle, her 1:1 Danielle had been removed and she was given another. They got along like a house on fire once again, but I genuinely believe she struggled with Delilahs needs. Delilah is complicated, her additional needs can be a lot to handle and understand. We have to give around the clock care, we need to be there to do all of her necessary care but also, stop her from itching her skin, keep an eye on her tremors and spasms to make sure she doesn't harm herself. It can be a lot, and it is very easy to feel out of your depth.

Shortly after the cracks had started to appear we had to make the hard decision to transfer Delilah to a new school. This wasn't necessarily the schools fault, they had tried their very best under the hardest circumstances. We weren't easy by any stretch of the imagination, we weren't awful either. We just wanted the best for our daughter and the school was out of their depth. We knew it, Delilahs team knew it and we just needed to reassure the school we knew it, but that we didn't hold it against them. They tried.

They now understood where we stood, how we felt and how difficult it was.

When it came to transferring Delilah we selected a school that had both a mainstream and medical provision. Delilah would start in the medical provision as her care needs were greater than her academical needs, this had become very apparent.

At her last meeting at her old school, where we would go over the last of the paperwork and forms, we explained our position. There was no ranting or raving, there was no short fuses. Just empathy. I understood where they stood, I knew it because I had been there once. I was given a task greater than I thought I'd ever be able to cope with, the difference being... I had no choice.

■■

A new school meant a new routine, and this school was roughly fifteen minutes away from our home. At the time of accepting Delilahs new placement we knew that this would be a bit of a struggle. Dan had returned to work and I would have to do all the school runs. I had only passed my driving test months beforehand and the idea of driving her back and forth was terrifying. Yet, the idea of Delilah taking local authority transport scared me even more.

I couldn't quite imagine putting Delilah in a cab every morning without the idea of what if something happened?? And I wasn't there to help her? What if, what if, what if?

It's a normal reaction to some times fear what you aren't aware of. Something you have never experienced before, so instead I took Delilah to school and brought her home. This worked great for the first couple of months until it got to a point where driving back and forth was exhausting. It was too much on top of everything else and I caved. I requested transport on a morning.

This actually became a saving grace I never expected. Delilah hated having her hair brushed so when we were running behind because of a meltdown I could just pop her into the cab whilst still in my pyjamas! Was I nervous at first? Of course I was, I was anxious and scared. I rang school each and every morning in order to know she arrived safe. This eased my mind and school never minded - Thankfully!

Now, we are two years on and Delilah takes the cab every morning and every evening. We have a wonderful cab driver that understands my concerns etc and each time they leave and Delilahs a bit upset, he will ring me because quite frankly, Delilahs a little.... Tinker.... She will get two minutes down the road and be absolutely fine. He will call and let me know this too.

Ive never felt panicked or nervous in a little while now, I can take my time on a morning and not get as stressed and on an evening I don't need to rush back from shopping etc to do school runs etc as she will be getting collected and dropped off.

Life is a little easier because of this service, it means Delilah gets to go to a school that is perfect for her needs and that I never have to worry about getting her there.

Mainstream or Special Needs schooling?

The question we will get asked a lot and a question we will ask ourselves a lot. It's not an easy one either.

So, which direction do you go? Quite frankly, no one can decide that but you and your family. What I would say is that I think everyone has an underlining idea of where they would like their child to go. For instance, I knew I wanted Delilah to go to a special needs school but listening to everyones opinions made me worry that it may not be the best route. Which in a way they were right, but so were we.

So my guide to finding the right school for your child is to follow these steps -

- View as many schools possible, both mainstream and special needs provisions. You will fall in love with some places and hate others, this will whittle your list down.

- Take into consideration travel. Is the school local to you? Are you able to drive or walk the school runs? How comfortable are you with transport provided by the Local authority? Knowing this will help you whittle down some schools too. If some schools are too far away and you have to consider school transport what are your views on that?

- Are they already in a nursery with friends? Can they transition with friends if they have made good bonds with other children?

- Where do your other children (if applicable) attend? Do you know the staff and would you feel they could care for your other child also?

- Think about restrictions you may have when applying for the school of your choice. Is this school realistically able to meet your Childs needs?

- Go back and visit again. If you are cautious, have questions or worried, make sure you express them. No one will fault you for having lots of questions and being concerned about your Childs placement. So go back and visit again and again. You know what is right.

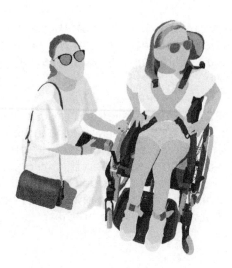

Delilah's Views On...
School

Hey bugs, How do you feel about your new school?
GOOD, it is very good for special people.

What do you like there?
I like my teachers and my friends.

How did you feel about having to leave your old school?
Erm, kind of sad because I liked my old school but it wasn't special enough for me. But I do miss my cousin that's there and my friends.

Do you feel like you fit in better at your new school?
Yes, because it has got more wheelchair people and at my old school I was the only one.

Do you understand why mammy and daddy changed you?
Yes, because I was the only one in a wheelchair or because it wasn't special enough.

Are you glad that we changed schools?
Kind of, but kind of not because I miss my friends and stuff.

How do you feel about taking a taxi to school?
Erm, I don't know because I kinda, its kinda bad, kinda of good, I don't like their jokes all the time, I would prefer to be with my mam and dad with my songs on the way to school.

Chapter **7**

SIBLING WORRY

The young carers...

Young carers, we all know the term, we have seen it on leaflets and posters in waiting rooms. We have also seen it being discussed on shows such as children in need and DIY sos. It has always been around but I think it has always been discussed when talking about children looking after their parent/parents or stepping in when there is a crisis within a family. But, for some kids being a young carer starts when a sibling is born. It doesn't matter whether the child is born before or afterwards there is a sense of care that is instantly ignited. We MUST care for our family, this is how it goes, siblings look after one another.

But these siblings are something else. They are resilient, patient and caring. They take the back foot and watch as their parents change. We deal with a lot when our children are born with additional needs and so do our other children. Where we may have somewhere or someone to discuss and express our concerns, our children do not. Our other children have to bottle up any fears and concerns for their sibling or parents until it overspills.

Both of my children that were born before Delilah have reacted it different ways throughout the last nine years. They have both been an absolute god-send and a nightmare equally. They are currently 16 and 13 in age and as you can imagine, teenagers... am I right??

■■

So, my eldest, my daughter. She was (still is) my princess, she was all things pink and fluffy and girly as a young child. A painfully shy little girl at times that wouldn't say boo to a goose! But, she loved to sing and dance around the house. Always watching something Hannah Montana or high school musical dreaming of being a star. When Delilah was born she was absolutely over the moon to have a little sister... she dreamt about pushing her in her pram, teaching her how to dance and showing her how to get around daddy when he would say no. But that didn't happen.

When Delilah was born, she was the best big sister! She doted on her endlessly, she would want to push her pram and lie on the floor on her back with her and look up to the ceiling with her whilst they both waffled stuff.

Hang on, I feel I need to give her a name, I feel I can't keep referring to her as 'she' or 'her'... but to keep her privacy as a teen I will call her Miley.

So, Miley was everything to Delilah, well, everything until Delilah discovered hair pulling of course. As Delilah grew up, Miley also did and the age gap seemed to grow massively between them. From playing dolls hours on end she was now fetching nappies, bottles and creams and lotions. Delilah could never be left alone, someone always had to be with her. So if I needed to wee or answer the door, I left it to Miley to just sit beside her and shout if she did anything she thought was 'weird'. I know, that sounds like a lot to put on a child. I know that it was probably 'wrong' maybe? I don't know... but Miley is eight years older than Delilah. She has always been a good kid... But I have always felt I failed her more. For a longer time there was just me and her, and then there was us and a whole lot of chaos.

So from that moment on Miley became a young carer, a helping hand for me and dad, a peace keeper when I wanted 5 minutes and a cuppa. She was more than she should have been at that age, and I know that.

I asked my daughter and son a couple of questions in order to get their perspective of being a young carer, their childhood and life in our family.

Teen Girl's Views...

How did you feel when mam and dad had another baby?

I was only little when Delilah was born so the idea of having a little sister was exciting because it had only been me, mam and *brother for as long as I can remember before dan came into my life.

How did you feel when we discovered that Delilah had additional needs? Can you even remember?

When we first found out Delilah had special needs I was confused and didn't really understand what was happening. I didn't understand what was happening. I didn't understand why she couldn't walker crawl like other kids could and why mam and dad were at hospital and doctor appointments a lot.

What so you think it means to be a carer & do you think you are a young carer?

To me being a young career means looking after someone you care about. I feel like I am a young carer because I try my best to help Delilah when she needs me and I have learnt not to take everything she says to heart because she doesn't mean it most of the time.

What do you feel growing up has been like in a special needs family?

Growing up in a special needs family has been hard because I didn't and still don't understand everything. However, there is new things and experiences that I wouldn't have had.

What do you think the hardest bit of our family is?

One of the hardest parts our family is probably being able to go places and spend time together. Sometimes it is hard for my mam and dad to get Delilah ready to go out because sometimes she doesn't want to have her hair brushed or to even go out at all.

What is one of you best memories growing up?

One of my best memories growing up was probably either when we went to centre Parcs or when we went to see Disney on ice because they were really amazing and I had always wanted to see Disney on ice since I was little.

Do you understand that when you were growing up that mam and dad had tried their very best for you all?

I understand how hard my mam and dad tried to make our lives as good as they could when we were growing up, even though it was hard sometimes.

Our son on the other hand, was much younger. My son was four years old when Delilah was born. As a boy, he wasn't particularly fussed about the screaming thing in the corner... he was more interested in trains and cars.

He - lets call him... what ridiculously embarrassing name can I give him... erm... Burt, let's call him Burt.

Burt had spent the next few years like that, almost in his own little world. He didn't care so much about the business of the house, or the fact I was tired. He was a boy, he wanted to play, especially with dad and he missed out often. Burt, like most boys wanted to be out often, to the park and climbing trees but I think my own down trodden thoughts and feelings had shattered that experience. I will always feel guilt for this, for them both missing so much.

For years Burt just plodded on, clearly upset at times over a missing mam and dad but overall just plodding on. It's only been during the last year id probably say it had a bigger impact on him. Due to the pandemic, we have had to be extra safe where others haven't. Take precautions where others maybe wouldn't so much, for him to see all this has been difficult. He's a good kid, but his frustrations can become clear often during school and at home. I can see it, I understand it too... I also get very frustrated at times.

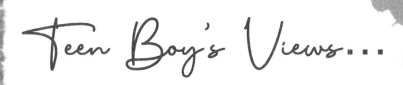

Teen Boy's Views...

How did you feel when mam and dad had another baby?

Happy and surprised.

How did you feel when we discovered that Delilah had additional needs? Can you even remember?

Can't remember.

What so you think it means to be a carer & do you think you are a young carer?

Yes and to care for people who are struggling, and support people with disabilities.

What do you feel growing up has been like in a special needs family?

Hard version of a normal family.

What do you think the hardest bit of our family is?

Trying to get Delilah out of the house.

What is one of you best memories growing up?

Being able to go out with my family and friends.

Do you understand that when you were growing up that mam and dad had tried their very best for you all?

Yes, I always knew if me, Leah or Delilah wanted something they would try their best.

Aww, a kid of many words...

What is a Young Carer?

A young carer is considered to be a person under the age of 18 who helps to look after a relative that has a disability, mental health condition, illness or issues with addiction.

Young carers are likely to look after a parent or parents or help look after a sibling. In the SEND community young carers are often considered to be helping their parents look after a sibling. The care that they give can be physical, such as running errands in the house such as fetching things, helping look after the child whilst their parents are in another room and helping to clean up etc. Young carers can also provide emotional support too, supporting both the child and parents.

You can gain more information on young carers rights on the NHS website, this covers the choice of having a young carers assessment also.

Young Carers Support...

There is a lot of young carers and sibling support available, the problem is it isn't as mainstream and clear as other support systems.

Accessing support services for your children, in your local area can really help create a space for your children to breath. I know that my children won't ever really tell me how much or how little they understand. They carry a lot on their shoulders unfortunately and none of which they asked for. The last thing they are going to do is tell me how much they are missing out or struggling to save my feelings. I found that encouraging my children along to our local carers centre really gave them some great peer to peer support. Support I couldn't give them for a good while.

The staff were very understanding, even when I felt like I had to over explain why I had missed a sports day or why we didn't visit the park as much as I would have liked. They never looked at me with judgment nor pity, they just told me not to worry, they were there to help and offer support to me and my children.

Which is exactly what they did.

Your child/children can also gain some wonderful support from their school also. By making their headteacher and staff aware they can provide extra support for your child and spot any signs of disruption or upset. Although school cannot take away homework and certain restrictions they can offer support to alleviate the pressure on the child.

Below I have done my best to find some great young carer support around the nation and not just restricted to the North east. If there isn't something here that suits you, your family or your area please reach out to your local carers centre. Parent carer forum or support services for advice.

Rather than applying links below to certain websites I have added the names of which I found to be supportive, a quick google and you would be able to find them!

Action for children

Barnardos

Carers Direct

Carers Trust

Carers UK

Family Action

Family Fund

KIDS

The Children's Society

Young Carers Festival

Young Minds

Also, check your local council or local offer website for more information.

Chapter 8

GONE, BUT YOUR NOT FORGOTTEN

One day they were there, next they were gone...

Delilah is now at school, we have her settled in her new school and although it wasn't an easy road, we got there in the end.

Unfortunately, at this point my mental health had already started to crumble and everything had come to a head.

You see when Delilah started nursery we were still in that stage of visiting every professional member of her team almost weekly. Delilah's team was pretty big to say the least and we were always meeting someone new and travelling in order to help diagnose her. A diagnosis that still hasn't come today, not that they haven't tried ...

But I started to feel abandoned, all of the professionals, all of the visitors and the constant run of appointments reduced massively. My days became a waiting game, waiting for phone calls, appointments and incidents at school that i'd need to step up for. This wasn't me, this wasn't my life, I'm a go-getter. I like to be busy and need to be busy. I hate to sit around doing nothing, it drives me insane.

So the feeling of abandonment was quite overwhelming. How can they all be here helping me one minute and gone the next? It felt like the first time I was actually expected to look after my child without support. I know i'm not the only one that has felt like this over time, I know i'm not alone and please know that you aren't either.

The thing is, this process is completely normal. It is normal to have a lot of intervention and then for it to dwindle off as the child starts school. It quite simply comes down to one thing.

You are now trained in the art of YOUR child. They, the professionals, have spent as much time as they can with you, showing you how to apply physio techniques, how to use equipment and how to look after your child to the best of your ability. They teach you all of the medical jargon, they try and point you in the right direction within regards to services and have to trust that you know your stuff, after all it is your child right?

So why do they not tell us this? Why is it that no one prepares us for it? Why doesn't someone say, "Hey, I know i've been here since your child started accessing our services but now that they are heading into school I will probably see you less, don't worry though, I will still be making visits in school and keeping update with their progress! And I am always at the end of the phone if you need me".

I think if we were pre-warned that this would be the case there wouldn't be as much of a shock, but instead we feel abandoned and alone, when in fact, we will never be alone.

■■

It is no secret that the SEND world is a difficult one to navigate. I have found that the best resources are that of other parents. Personally, I really struggled to fit in with other parents for a long while. I think this comes down to the fact I always felt like a bit of a fraud. I always felt as if we were in no way shape, or form, struggling as much as others. Was our life difficult? Yes, of course but I always felt like it could have been worse. Delilah was at one point being considered for a feeding tube, fortunately she proved she could do without it, and yet had to carry a suction machine around as she was constantly creating saliva and aspirating. As a parent I obviously compared the both and deemed the feeding tube to be clearly the more upsetting option. So of course I saw those families who had relied on them as having a lot more to contend with.

It wasn't until I became friends with some families who had these difficulties to contend with I found that they also compared their lives to others. It was a never ending circle. I once had a conversation with a mum who's child couldn't speak at all, she felt that we had it harder as Delilah could. Of course, I listened patiently as she explained that although her child couldn't speak she would hate to have to hear how they felt. How she would hate to have to answer the questions that I had to answer along the way. This blew my mind, but I understood where she was coming from.

As people, human beings even, we often compare even when we don't want to. We can't help it, I don't know the science behind it and I won't pretend to, but what I do know is that, this is how the world works and revolves. Between sympathy, empathy and jealousy, we are always comparing. And in my case it has never been in malicious, just never felt I could complain, or ask for help. As if I was taking up time that could be used better else where and given to someone else.

Once I did start speaking to other parents I started to really hear I wasn't alone. That we were entitled to help and there was help available for us. I just had to ask for it.

Parent carer forums are a great source of information in your area and should be able to point you in the direction of a good coffee group. Quite often they will also have a private group on social media that will allow you to speak to other like minded parents and make connections. Usually the best source of information on service's and events is other parents.

I decided to write this book to empower parents, to hopefully not allow them to get to the point where I once did. So, look for your parent carer forum, your local SENDIASS (also known as special educational needs and disability information and support service, phew, think that's long to read try saying it as often as I do!) Or at your local carers centre. All of these will help you with questions and queries. Don't feel nervous about second guessing or questioning someone, after all this Is your child. Don't feel worried about expressing that you are struggling, some of the strongest people do. And never feel ashamed about applying for funding.

■■

What is a parent carer forum?

What is a parent carer forum?

The way parent carers work with professionals is by forming groups called parent carer forums.
A parent carer forum is a group of parents and carers of disabled children. Their aim is to make sure the services in their area meet the needs of disabled children and their families.
They do this by gathering the views of local families and then working in partnership with local authorities, education settings, health providers and other providers to highlight where local services, processes and commissioners are working well, or challenge when changes or improvements need to be made.
In England there are parent carer forums in almost all local authority areas. See public contact details for the parent carer forums in England.
Forums usually have a steering group of parents who lead this work and listen to the views of other parents in the local area to make sure they know what is important to them. Forums are keen to hear from as many parent carers as possible.

Who can join a parent carer forum?

Parents or carers of a child with any type of additional need or disability are welcome to join. Joining your forum does not mean you have to commit lots of time. In most forums you can join and receive information, and then decide if you want to get more involved at your own pace.

There are some wonderful charities out there for funding for equipment, short breaks and household help. Applying for funding doesn't make you any less of a parent. If anything give yourself a pat on the back for reaching out and also, filling out all that paperwork! When applying for equipment etc make sure you speak to your physiotherapist or occupational therapist first. Obviously you know what you want for your child, but the likelihood is that you may need a supporting letter to help towards funding, so have a meeting with those and do plenty of research. You don't want another big piece of equipment in your home to take up even more space do you?

Short breaks, local councils sometimes have their own caravan that is accessible through application for a short stay. If not, there is charities that do enable you to access funding for a family stay somewhere, tickets to theme parks and days out. These are designed to bring the whole family together, they understand the importance of siblings and the divide that can happen.

Funding for household equipment is also able to be applied for through selected charities. This is to help support you, the parents, especially when unexpected accidents and issues occur. We once had to apply to family fund because our cooker went pop one day and although my husband works, who has the disposable income to pull out for a brand new cooker a month before Christmas? Yep, Christmas... it was another day, another drama.

To help you find funding I would advise a quick google and you will come across such pages as disability-grants.org which will help you find the grant's you are looking for.

Asking for help and extra financial support does not make you any less of anything. The taboo of asking for help is gone in the SEND world and you're never very far from someone who has applied for something. You will probably meet some others that will happily tell you where they are applied, what for and how easy or difficult the process was.

Don't worry about judgment, just do what is best for your family.

Other support networks for Parent Carers

Amongst parent carer forums there is other charities and organisations set up in order to help support parent carers. I have added below the very supportive services for parents carers.

Contact - for families with disabled children. If you haven't already heard of contact, you probably will soon. Contact was an organisation set up over 40 years ago by families of children with disabilities, their most common similarities were that they are had common experiences within the SEND world. After coming together they really understood the importance of supporting one another... and this still stands now.

Contact are there to support families throughout their journey of SEN or SEND. Offer parents the opportunity of programmes and training that they wouldn't be offered elsewhere and strongly believe in parent carer participation.
They have a wonderful handbook, website and social media pages including a closed group for friendship and support.

Carers Assessment. Every parent carer is entitled to a carers assessment. This assessment is carried out via the disability social workers team. This isn't your average social worker, so don't be afraid of the idea they are coming to take your children away, as that is not the case.

The carers assessment is designed to help figure out what type of support would best help you and your family. This could be to help provide respire, direct payments or help with your well being.

I have found our Disability social worker to be an absolute god send, although this may not be always the case.

Family Fund. Family fund are an organisation and charity that has been set up to not only support families well being through their resources on their website but to offer funding towards crucial support. This funding could be awarded in grants for short stays and holidays, or items for helping at home. Such as, garden play, play equipment or household goods.
Family fund can be accessed through their website online.

Grant Tips

Apply to the right charity-
Make sure you meet the criteria of that charity to save disappointment.

Be as in-depth as you can-
Make the application about your child/your family or your situation and not generic.

Be honest-
Specify exactly what you need and why you need it, this gives the charity a good picture of the application.

Evidence -
Don't forget the evidence! Supporting letters help a lot, especially from your paediatrician, therapist, and others.

Can you help?-
Ask yourself whether you can contribute towards it, could you do some fundraising and show that you are trying to contribute?

Timescales -
Check the timescales, if you are in a rush there is often charities to help accommodate this. Otherwise, check the application time's and process times as some may take longer than others.

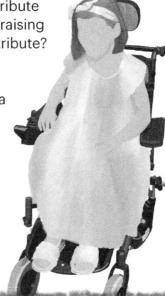

Chapter 9

IF WE SURVIVE THIS, IT WILL BE A MIRACLE

Relationship struggles, silences and snooze buttons

Myself and Dan have been together for over twelve years. To say that it has been easy would be a lie, it's been more like a rollercoaster that has some bits where it has been super scary, tense but also some bits where we have done nothing but giggle.

Just like any normal relationship right?

Except our relationship went from your average age old story of man goes to work, woman looks after the children and has tea on the table to a scene from a paranormal activity movie where there is something going on in the house but no one has a fucking clue what it is.

Also, someone is always leaving the lights on around the house... and its not ghosts DAN.

Our relationship didn't have an easy start, it was difficult to open myself up to the prospect of allowing someone come in and help. I had been alone a while and I was an independent woman...(cue destiny's child)... So every time he took a step forward I took a step back. Until one day about a year in, it just clicked, we figured it all out and we were good.

■■

Delilah arrived almost four years after.

Being Special Needs parents really takes it out of you in so many ways. We have days where we don't talk and days where we talk about everything. I mentioned earlier on in the book that it was the first drive home where we didn't say a word. That is still the case now. When we have been to an appointment that has been very trying, nerve-racking or particularly worrying it can really take it out of you. There is stuff, obviously, that you want or need to discuss. Such as hospital stays, procedures and medications that just simply have to wait. They have to wait because we have to process it ourselves. We have learnt very quickly that diving straight into a conversation after leaving can sometimes just cause more harm than good. We nod away to said professional, wave and say "see you next time!" then jump in the car and remain silent. Which is completely bazaar...but not so much after a while.

Later that evening we will discuss the days events, it can lead to tears, on my part usually and a very clear headed dan talking me down. Or sometimes it can be an argument. We don't always agree you see, not with each other or the professionals. It can be a fight against each other, where he will have concerns I necessarily don't have but he won't have chosen to ask you know the ACTUAL professional and instead may have kept quiet and allowed me to do all the talking as usual. Sometimes he will side with professionals views and I may want to wait it out or see other options. This will mean that I will try and win because I do the majority of the care. When in reality we both just want what is right for our child.

Relationships are all about compromise among other things, but when you become parents of a special little one, compromise will become something you will do daily.

Not only did we have to compromise on all of your average day discussions, we had to compromise on our time together and apart. When we were together it was who would change nappies or care and who would clean up and look after our other children. When we tried to go out without the kids (very, very rare) we would compromise on who would have a few drinks and who would be 'on call'. Then we reached a point where Delilah was established at school and it felt as if one of us should really take the opportunity and get a job, get some normality back. So off dan went.

Then it was just me and Delilah most of the time, then the older kids after school.

■■

It's weird because there is a conversation that you kinda want to have but nobody ever wants to approach, which to me is absolutely madness right? Like if we are going to talk about it ALL and how our life has changed we have to discuss the next bit. Not just because I want to share, because trust me I do not but I know this bit will help someone.

Our sex life... or intimacy... let's say intimacy it sounds nicer!

Yup, you read that right... here we go. Can you remember when you first give birth and the midwives say 'no hanky panky for **SIX** weeks!' And you're like " that's no problem because i've just pushed a 9lb 3oz baby out of my downstairs and he's getting nowhere near it!".

Well, getting intimate after discovering your child has additional needs is a lot like that after birth timescale.

It maybe the last thing you ever want to do. I know for me personally, that it wasn't even a thought for a good while. I was not only exhausted from all of the new big words I was learning and all of the day to day running of the house and looking after the kids I was slowly recoiling into myself a little. It was a lot to take in and I couldn't even consider it. Which was strange as we had a relatively good sex life before! (Sorry mam, dad, anyone that actually knows me!)

It wasn't just me though, dan understood he could see it. He could see that it just wasn't going to happen no matter how much he was missing me. After all intimacy brings couples together, it's a loving act... no matter how quick it is haha... but it bonds you together for a little while. It's just you and your partner sharing a moment.

So, don't give up. If you were intimate beforehand, take your time, don't rush it and come back to it when you're ready. Your partner will support you regardless and no doubt feel the same way. Just like after birth.

■■

At different times, sometimes the same time our mental health has suffered. There is a greater impact on you personally other than physically. Some parent carers do suffer a degree of PTSD, depression and anxiety regarding the diagnosis or non diagnosis of their child.

For dan and I we have both felt the pressure of the SEND world both physically and mentally. I have already spoke at length about my anxiety and issues. I will ALWAYS have mental health issues now, the extent I had suffered will never leave me but I do feel 100 times better than I was. Physically the aches and pains from lifting and handling are something else right? I feel most days I need a zimmer frame just to get up at the ripe old age of 33! I started to go to gym recently to keep not only my mental health fit but my body moving. Turns out if you sit longer than half an hour you seize up....18 month of a pandemic really made this clear.

Dan, himself went through a stage of feeling lost and alone. We don't talk about dads enough I feel. Dan does talk now, he is also encouraging people to talk about being a carer at work and I think this is amazing. Just because he goes to work doesn't mean he isn't a carer. He is my rock at the end of the day when I want to vent, or run out and hide in the car for a bit while crying or screaming at the end of a pier.

Imagine, heading off to work everyday knowing that your wife was having a breakdown, was always so busy with three children and a home to run and yet, bills needed to be paid. Leaving now would land us in arrears we may never recover from. So he persevered, he stuck in at work and when at home helped in anyway he could and in anyway

Delilah would allow. Then physically, wow did it impact him physically.

It was the 7th of September 2017, me and dan had a little falling out the night before nothing major just a stupid disagreement. Dan had to taken my dad to work through a friends house and then drop L off at school on the way home. He never gave any indication that something wasn't right but to be honest that's Dan all over he never tells me anything haha. Anyway off he went, about an hour or so later he returned looked round the sitting room door and said "I don't feel right". His heart was beating too fast it was irregular and he was getting an uncomfortable feeling in his chest which was causing him to be short of breath. After a nerve wracking phone call to the NHS 111 line because Dan wouldn't just go straight to the hospital like a normal person, we were advised to go to A&E "surprise, surprise". Dan had to drive us to hospital, not because we couldn't get an ambulance, because we could have, but he refused. He drove because at the time I couldn't. That day was the first day where I was ushered out of the room so that he could be defibrillated.

After hours awaiting his heart to go not only back into rhythm but also slow down, he needed intervention. He was covered in wires and had a drip placed in his arm, something I had never seen with him before. Something I'd seen with Delilah, yes... but never dan. I sat there for hours while he was exhausted and head spinning, while he was constantly being checked and monitored. I was a nervous wreck. I did the one thing he hated. I rang his mam. Someone else needed to be here, she needed to know. He hates to worry anyone, he hates to ask for help, which is that very stereotypical vision we see of men. The stereotype that here, up north is very much still apparent and dominant.

Anyway's, I was ushered off into a horrible, horrible bereavement room. You know, the room with the white walls, the little side table and the 'supposed to be comfy but not comfy sofas' and I sat there. Alone. While they slowed his heart down to a stop then defibrillated him to kick it back into shape. "It will take less than five minutes!" They said... and I was still sat here twenty minutes later. Liars.

I had updated everyone I knew then rang my friend. She was lush, she kept me calm, made me laugh and made me feel more positive whilst awaiting Dans mam.

Once the nurse came to retrieve me I headed back into the room expecting my ever so sarcastic husband who thinks he is hilarious telling some sort of hilarious joke about going to the other side... instead he was there lifeless, still completely out and wired up. I sobbed my heart out. This was my rock, this was the guy that although never agrees with me, knows I am always right. He is the one who persevered when I tried to dump him X amount of times, he was the guy who consoled me on the tough days and celebrated with me on the good days. He was the dad to my three kids. I was guttered.

Once we got him home he was on rest for a little while until we could get some medications and discover how best to treat this in the future. He was diagnosed with atrial fibrillation. From then on his life had changed, he was more tired, more cautious and we were always awaiting the next episode. Which he has had, a good few times now.

I want to tell you the worst thought that ran through my mind when this happened. I want to share it because I promised to be honest and to discuss it all. My worst thought was this, I can't cope if he doesn't 145 recover from this. If he had left us, I wouldn't know what to do. I can't cope with all of this and more alone. It is just not an option.

No matter how much he does my nut in.

■■

Thankfully, those episodes are now far and few between and he has returned to work full-time. Although Dan can't be a driver anymore he is now training to be a manager, he loves it and you can see that although our life and his medications to control his heart make him exhausted, he is happy. That makes me happy.

His work has been fantastic, you don't realise how many rights you have in the workplace as carers because they aren't so openly discussed that often, but as carers we do have rights.

Not only have they changed his times and days they have been very supportive and understanding when it has came to leaving work on a whim for Delilah.

Your Rights As a Carer at Work...

Working parents of children with disabilities (under the age of 18) have the right to request flexible working arrangements. You also have a statutory right to ask your employer for flexible working if you care for an adult who is a relative or lives at the same address as you.

Carers also have the right to take unpaid time off work for dependants in an emergency. Returning to work after being a carer may have an impact on any entitlements and benefits you receive as a carer. The amount of hours you do, how much you earn and your   savings will be taken into consideration.

For more information on carers right's within the workplace please check out the NIdirect.org website for more information and support, along with some really useful links.

Chapter 10

WHO EVEN AM I?

Finally, a bit about me...

So, who even are you? I hear you ask... well after all of the last nine chapters, I am still just mam. I know, I will drive others crazy for stating I am 'just' a mam but to me I am a mam first and carer second. That doesn't at all downsize the role we all play and it certainly won't change the opinion of masses that we have been trying to convince that what we do is hard AT ALL. To me I am mam, I'm not Tracey, the one who used to have nights out on a weekend, simply because I don't get the opportunity. I am now the counselling college student and hopefully If all goes well... author, rather than the lost mess I used to be who couldn't quite figure out what exactly she wanted to do with her life. I am all of this and more.

I am a cook, a cleaner, a decorator, a laundromat, a dog sitter, a fixer of small things, a dish washer and a snack bitch (also known as servant).

I am also a physiotherapist, a PA, an occupational therapist, a nurse, a chemist, a masseuse, a spoon feeder, a security guard, a teacher, a speech and language therapist, a nappy changer, a researcher, a counsellor, a dresser and a safety blanket.

I am all of this and more because I had to be. There was no choice or alternative, don't get me wrong, I tried to give her away... but they kept bringing her back...

Don't be offended I was joking... kinda!

But we are all those things and more. We are our children's worlds. Think of it this way, when you are fighting for equipment, funding or adaptions... did your child ask you to do that? Because mine certainly didn't. My child asks for red crisps and her iPad. That's it, we do everything that we do for our children because we love them, they are ours and we are gonna fight tooth and nail for them at whatever the cost.

That's what we do. We have to, because if we don't who on earth will?

So whatever you call yourself, or see yourself a carer, mam, dad or an alien for all I care... you can do this. I am still standing. Others before me are still standing.

We are a little broken, a little bruised but we live to fight another day. Your down days won't always be around and up days are just around the corner.

These up days may not be on the level of your friends and their kids but that is ok. Don't beat yourself up too much about comparing, or being jealous of another Childs abilities over your own. We have all had them thoughts, not everyone likes to admit it, but I will.

You will struggle, or have struggled. Push through it, the best quote I ever did see was ' you can't go around it, you have to go through it ' and this kind of sums up the world of SEND parenting. You will go through so many different emotions on a daily basis for a while... and I can't promise you that it get's easier or better, because I would be lying.

It get's... tolerable. You learn to cope with your ever changing life style. One day you wake up and you are in a routine, may feel like groundhog day some days but not every day. You will have your shit figured out, you will know who your people are and who aren't. You will know all of your Childs team and who to turn to and when. All of this? This will be you smashing it. Wont feel like it, trust me, but you are. To everyone else you are super mam, a warrior and something to be inspired by. To you? You're frantically treading water while looking like you've got it all together. And that? That is real special needs parenting.

"Once you learn to appreciate the small victories there's no need for a finish line"

■■

When I went to counselling, it was the best thing I ever did. From day one when I walked in that room I knew I had made the right decision. I couldn't cope with not talking about it anymore and needed to speak freely. Once I'd sat down and got comfortable in my first session my counsellor asked "so what has brought you here?"

I had no fucking clue... I needed help, that was clear. I was lashing out to people I loved or hibernating. I had given up on trying and instead was getting by just coping.

I proceeded to say I wasn't sure... then all of a sudden, I couldn't shut up. I let it all out, the fact that no two weeks were the same, the fact I felt so guilty about the care I have to give one child over my other children and how I had tried so hard to help others with a group that I had to walk away from because I had felt like a fraud.

I had been part of a trio of mams who set up a coffee group and play groups in the summer for children with all needs and their siblings. There was nothing like this in our area and it was completely needed... it started off just an idea from a friend and then she ended up dragging me and another into it. We were inseparable... the problem was though, they seemed to be smashing it. They seemed to have all their ducks in a row and I seemed to be lacking behind. This went on for just over a year when I had to give in and walk away. My anxiety was taking a hold of me again and I felt as if I wasn't even a second thought, whatever the group was gonna do, it was going to be done regardless of whether I was there or not and I was hurt. So I left, I left to figure my shit out and get help. Which I did.

So, back to counselling. My counsellor was brilliant, she told me I had a reactive lifestyle, this meant that every time we got into a routine and something got tipped upside down I was having to adjust and react accordingly. It totally made sense! I never get settled and although I don't always fear the worst, I am always on guard 'just in case'. This way I don't feel to uprooted if it does go tits up. Once we had what felt like a million sessions, I had made a lovely friend and had changed my view on my life and how I will deal with things in the future.

She also told me not to hide my light under a bushel... which I had to google and now i'm here writing this book, so thanks Deb.

I wasn't against seeking counselling, I needed it. I needed to change my mindset and seek help and it certainly wasn't as scary as I thought it was going to be. There was no lying down while someone was tapping there pen and asked me how I was feeling... granted a lie down would have been nice as those hours were my only escape but it wasn't what I had built it up to be. It was a literal life saver... but it had to be done at the right time. It had to be when I was ready and open to it or else I don't think it would have helped as much as it did.

So now I'm fixed! Jokes, I will never be fixed. I will always have mental health issues, i've not met a SEND parent that hasn't to date (not to say there isn't any out there) but at least I am ok. That's the best we can ask for right?

But to others? I am supermum, something to be envied as I must have it all together, but I still don't... and that's ok.

The idea that having a child with additional needs must make me some sort of extra super being is hilarious to me, I'm not a super mum just doing my best like any other parent would. I appreciate the thought when it is said to me, but it is soo far off what I actually am some days.

■■

So what do I do to keep myself sane? I walk, I take long walks, alone usually and have my headphones in with some good music. This makes me happy. I try and take Zumba classes and things... I know, so cliché but it genuinely does help your mindset if you move a little. You don't have to run a marathon or sign up to a gym, stick a leotard on and bust out some moves to some *Hoe Sticks... couldn't write his name just incase, you know, copyright and that! There is no rules to this, do what you want when you want to keep your mental health ticking over, trust me you will feel good for it.

I also have started to write, I know this isn't for everyone at all and you don't need to share it but writing can help. I now write blogs and have a website. I am trying to empower other parents to get the right help etc from early on, hence the book...

I am trying my best not to be like everyone else, to offer something different and down to earth. I don't believe in baffling people with big words but instead just being myself. I am happy to say i'm struggling out loud when its too much but also to brag from the rooftops when something finally goes my way, it's balance right?

Also, I swear. I know not everyone will approve and that's ok, not everyone will understand me or like me and that's fine. Each to their own and all that... but those parents who aren't spending their days doing homework on the big words and seminars need to know that it's ok to be just winging it... same goes for those that are the opposite. We are all different, all in different scenarios but all doing our best.

■■

I am now starting to see where I can carve time for me, not just carve the time but make the time for me. For instance, this book, going to the gym and within the last year I finished my level two in counselling and introduction into caring for babies and young children. I was keen to complete these courses as essentially this is the sector I want to be in. I want to work helping and supporting other parents, because I am one. The people we tend to meet are trained in our lives. They take courses and tests in order to help support us. We appreciate them, of course, but it doesn't beat someone that has lived in experience does it? After all, who knows better?

So that is where I am at in my journey. I have left LOADS out of this book, but as a first book I don't think it's too bad now is it?

It has been a wonderful experience for me, to write the book. My story, my words, for you. If you knew me I'd like to think you could hear my horrendous accent come through every word that you have read. The fact that I have a no wholes barred stance and then maybe you'd understand why my nickname is trigger...

If you have enjoyed the book (and let's face it, why wouldn't you enjoy reading someone else's train wreck of a life?) Then please head over to our website and our social media pages.

We are The SEND world according to me... Because this is my view on our world.

Cape

She lay down her cape,
raised her hands and said,
"I'm struggling".
She couldn't and didn't
want to hold it altogether
anymore.
She shared her story of
struggle, of grief and the
feeling of failure.

Others joined her, they took off
their capes, they all shared their
stories and struggles.

She wasn't alone.

By Me...

I think we all look back on a time of our life and wish we could send ourselves a heads up or a clue to what was coming our way.

I have thought about it a couple of times and I think these are the 20 things I wish I could have told myself...

1. It will be ok. It won't always be ok, but at times it will fan-fucking-tastic... and sometimes it will just suck.

2. You didn't expect this when you dreamt about these years whilst pregnant, but you will make the most of them.

3. You are doing your best, you haven't failed, you haven't let anyone down, if anything, they are prouder of you more now than ever before.

4. This was not your fault, although you think it is and the guilt is very overwhelming, it turns out Delilahs skin was dan's fault, not yours so blame him.

5. Start training now, in 8 years time your back is going to be knackered, you will be considering hip surgery and everyone will tell you to JUST hoist because it's quicker... it is NEVER quicker... but less painful.

6. She will find her voice and start speaking, don't you worry about that!

7. She won't walk, she never will but she will love announcing to people when out on a walk that she wants to go home as her 'leg's are tired from all this walking'... and remember shouting at a disabled child in public is frowned upon... but you will learn to not care about that also.

9. She will get your dry sense of humour. Don't worry, she will be able to defend herself and EVERY LIVING CREATURE EVER. Which

although is great, can be very exhausting when constantly arguing with her to not get any extra pet's.

10. Mainstream school is not the way to go, listen to the 602 people that told you otherwise and head straight to provision. Save yourself a headache.

11. She will eat also, granted only beige foods due to her ASD diagnosis and stock up on red crisps. You can NEVER be without red crisps, got it? This is very important.

12. Dan will be amazing, trust him. He has your back, always. Although you seem very separated right now, you will be stronger than ever. Killing him and burying his body will only pop up a few times.

13. There is NO shame in counselling, seeking help or screaming fuck this! At the top of your lungs... unless you are in a public place then it's super frowned upon. You find this out too.

14. Sarcasm can help, but stop telling strangers who politely state " I don't know how you do it " that you tried abandoning her on a neighbours step, they don't appreciate it... although their reaction IS hilarious.

15. Find some good friends. Especially ones as messed up as you.

16. There is no diagnosis in the world that will change your situation, this is something you learn to live with as it is not the be all and end all.

17. Her scaly skin will be a nightmare, incredible itchy and shed EVERYWHERE. But also... she is a gross kid who will pick the skin sheaths off and hand them to you in public... she has zero shame.

18. You are so not alone. You think you are but you're not, but at some point in the future you will wish you were.

19. Enjoy those baby nappies with little poops! You will be happy to do all of them so you can cash in the post-new-medication diarrhoea nappies with Dan as you can say 'i've changed them for years'.

20. Lastly trust YOUR instincts, trust your gut, trust your team. You don't think you're made of strong stuff, you don't think you can do this but you can. You can do it all and will... plus extra.

You're made of strong stuff Tracey, don't you fucking forget it.

Dear Professionals,

The last nine years have been difficult for our family, and for all families in your care. I am sure you know this as I am positive you have seen it hundreds of times.

Except, you don't see it all.

You don't physically see the impact it has on a family, how could you within the twenty minutes of an appointment or a visit? You can't see that my teenage children after nine years of tears, meltdowns and difficulty resort to often sitting upstairs in their room. We have to coax them out to spend time with us, granted it hasn't always been this way but this is where they are currently at. You don't see the impact this life has on siblings, the role they take that they didn't ask for.

You don't see the strain it has on a couples relationship, the days we have sat in silence after receiving bad news, the heated discussions when we have not seen eye to eye on treatment plans or school choices. It is now left to me, it's me that makes the final decision and who signs all of the paperwork because I don't work, I can't work, Delilah is home more than she is at school. There is slim job prospects for carers like me.

You don't see that when you fit our home with equipment, drop off equipment or tell us to give something a try that this is an adjustment. Especially, in those early days... imagine being told the difficulties your child will face in life then have your home filled with scary equipment in order to care for them. These are often in black and grey colours too... not fun, reassuring or appealing to children.

*Listen to us when it comes to adaptions and sleeping arrangements. This is our **home** it's a home we created for **all** of our family.*

You don't see the impact it has across our families, on either side. We used to be close knit, now I barely see my family or Dans. The belief that they may offend or upset, or think we won't show up as their children are able to do things our children can't. There is an atmosphere you can't see but can feel, a pity or a feeling as if we somehow have it lucky and get more attention... trust me, we don't.

You don't see the changes parents have to take when it comes to work. Sacrificing jobs they trained hard for, to take jobs with less hours that they don't like but loath.

You didn't see me the day my husband had to be defibrillated, because his heart had taken on the strain of our life to a point where it couldn't take anymore. He is now on medication for life, and looking at the possibility of heart surgery.

You didn't see me and all the others when we had to start counselling to deal with all of the above and more. I was sat in a room where I was asked "what brought you here today?" And I didn't know where to start. Could it be the strain on my family? My marriage? The feeling of lost when i'm alone? The reality of this is life now.

You didn't see all the tears that have been shed, from all parents, carers, everywhere.

Please stop telling us that funding isn't available for XY & Z... we don't care, we want the best care, the best equipment and support if possible.

Please don't end appointments with "we are just at the end of the phone if you need us" then make it incredibly hard to get in touch with you.

Please don't fill us with terminology that we don't understand, then tell us not to google it. Either use layman's terms or help us understand better.

Our children aren't projects. They aren't 'work' to us.

And finally, why is everything a fight? Why do we fight for necessary needs for our children. Other parents don't fight for school, accessibility or support?

Work with us to create proper early intervention and support.

Now, none of this is your fault at all, and this letter is certainly not saying that. This letter is from me to you, asking you to remember all of the above and more before you consider sending us on another road trip to London, to try more equipment, to try medications with side effects, or ask me to hold her down while you sedate her for surgery. We appreciate you, we trust you in the decisions you make, we literally put our children's lives in your hands and allow you to guide us on this crazy journey we had no choice being on.

I just want you to stop for a second every time your next appointment is due in and think, no matter what number patient they are that day, everyone struggles. Most parent carers don't get sleep they are exhausted, listen to them. Some of them are silently crying out for someone to step in but won't say so because of the fear that they will be shamed for struggling, hear them.

We know you have a huge job on your hands, we know you see thousands of families...

But each time you see one, you are seeing one, their family and their story. Take a moment and remember although you may have helped us learn this life, it didn't get easier. We appreciate you, all that you have done and more.

Sincerely,

Delilah's Mam

Tracey

ACRONYMS

Ever get confused with the acronyms on your letters and forms?
Don't fear, here is your handy quick guide to what all those letters mean!

ADD attention deficit disorder
ADHD attention deficit hyperactivity disorder
AS Asperger syndrome
ASC autistic spectrum condition
ASD autistic spectrum disorder
BESD behavioural, emotional and social difficulties
BSL British Sign Language
CAF common assessment framework
CAMHS Child and Adolescent Mental Health Services
CIN Child in Need PP
CoP Code of Practice
CP child protection
CYP children and young people
DDA Disability discrimination act
DLA Disibility Living Allowance
EAL English as an additional language
EBD Emotional and Behavioural Difficulties
ED. P Educational Psychologist
EHCP Education health care plan
EP Enhanced provision
EYFS Early years Foundation Stage
EWO Educational welfare officer
FAS Fetal Alcohol syndrome

FASD Fetal alcohol spectrum disorders
FSM free school meals
GDD Global developmental delay
HFA High functioning Autism
HI hearing impaired
HLTA higher level teaching assistant
IEP individual education plan
IRP independent review panel
LAC looked after children
LARM locality allocation and review meeting
LD Learning disability
LDD learning difficulties and disabilities
LO local offer
LSCB local safeguarding children board
MA Multi-agency
MARAG multi agency referral action group
MLD Moderate learning difficulty
NAS National Autistic Society
NT Neurotypical
ODD Oppositional defiant disorder
OT Occupational therapist
PDA Pathological demand avoidance
PECS Picture exchange communication system

PEP Personal education plan (for looked after children)
Personal learning plan

PMLD Profound and multiple learning difficulties pupil premium

PSHE Personal, social and health education
RAD Reactive attachment Disorder

RAISEonline Reporting and Analysis for Improvement through School Self Evaluation

SLT or (SALT) speech and language therapy

SDQ strengths and difficulties questionnaire

SEAL social and emotional aspects of learning

SEN Special Educational Needs

SEND Special educational needs and disabilities

SENCo special educational needs coordinator

SLCN speech, language and communication needs

SLD severe learning difficulty

SLT school leadership team

SM selective mutism (formerly known as elective mutism)

SLD specific learning difficulty

SPDs sensory processing disorders

SS Social Services

START Statutory Assessment Resources Team

SW Social Worker

TA Teaching assistant / teacher assessment

TAC team around the child

TAF team around the family (when CAF is about whole family)

TFC together for children

TFF Together for Families

VI visually impaired

There maybe others i've missed, if so google is your friend and if in doubt always ask a medical professional!

So that's it, if you got this far well done you! I regret nothing.

This is my very first book, it probably won't be my last either! Next I really want to try my hand at a kid's book which I think will be fun.

I want to thank...

My wonderful other half, he hasn't half put up with some crap... from me and Delilah... but mainly Delilah.

My two wonderful kids who have become carers, even though they didn't ask to be. I love you...

To the family that stuck by us.

My wonderful friends, you know who you are.

To Julie Hemmer, the first to support us.

To the medical professionals who have helped us with Delilah and her journey.

To the 'professionals' that became life long friends.

To those who supported me on the project and told me I could do wonderful things.

To those that read my blog and aren't sick of my shit yet,

I'll be back...

Printed in Great Britain
by Amazon